Mattsen

Is It Friday Already?

Nottzen

Is It Friday Already?

By Greta Rasmussen

ISBN 0-936110-00-7
Library of Congress Catalog Card Number: 79-92710
Copyright ©1980 by Greta Rasmussen
All rights reserved. Printed in the U.S.A.

Tin Man Press
Box 219
Stanwood, Wa. 98292 TIN
MAN
PRESS

Contents

Introduction

This is a learning center book for teachers who are skeptical, and rightly so, of learning centers. It is for *good* teachers who want more—more learning, more control, more satisfaction, more rapport with students, more fun and *more* going on in their classrooms.

In this book are more than 250 carefully-developed learning projects which have been used in a third-grade classroom. There is also a week-by-week systematic plan which shows how to use this program. Its implementation should be relatively easy because it requires only the most basic of materials.

This book is *not* for those teachers who like antonym boats, competitive progress charts, right answers and smiley faces. This book does not contain the usual learning center tricks. You will not find a single Humpty Dumpty egg divided into two parts, the one bearing the prefix in search of the other with the base word, a task which can be accomplished by most children in three minutes, reinforcing an already too-short attention span and producing in students a dangerous faith in their genius!

Similarly, there will be no creative writing tasks instructing the child to tell the teacher about the night all his toys talked. Because what child *really* wants publicly to anthropomorphize the teddy bear which has been an important part of his private life?

Nor will there be any assignments asking the child to write about the time all the fleas left the flea circus (what child knows what a flea circus is anyway?), or instructions to design a dandruff machine for lions. These projects, made in the name of creativity, espouse the *lowest* form of creativity—and most children are not easily fooled.

We should instead give children tasks which are within the perimeters of their own interests and experience.

It is a common assumption that learning centers, in addition to providing the "creative" experience, should reinforce skills taught in the regular curriculum, which is another way of saying that centers should serve a purpose for the teacher. A learning center, according to conventional wisdom, is a well-defined area in a classroom where pupils work independently with materials which teach, reinforce or enrich a group of skills.

This definition is too narrow.

Everyone knows that a large part of teaching is spent in practice or review, because repetition is essential to learning. However, when a student finishes his regular work and has free time and the teacher sends him to a center, is it any wonder he is turned off by what he finds—more practice, review and repetition?

Learning centers should not be platforms for teacher propaganda, for endless skillwork or for mindless imagining in the name of creativity. Rather, they should be staging areas for students to *escape* from some of the necessary school rigidity into areas of meaningful mental and physical play. This is not to say centers should exist as places for students to "do their own thing." In this system, there is a definite structure, the components of which follow.

1. *All students in the room use the centers.* Why should centers be only for the "bright" or the ones who finish regular work the most quickly? If the centers are truly concerned with projects requiring reflective thought, if they are places where Piagetian and problem-solving tasks are going on, then *all* students should be beneficiaries. Does an "average" or "poor" student need this exposure any less? I found, indeed, that the opposite was true, that the lower students were the most enthusiastic about going to the centers and that perhaps their progress was the greatest when you think of where they had been all these years—in their seats getting it right!

2. *The centers are mandatory.* Ideally, they shouldn't have to be, but human nature doesn't work that way. No matter how good your centers are, when they are used voluntarily they will be ineffectual. This should come as no surprise. When the choice is yours, which do you read, Spinoza or McCall's?

To some extent, it is our job as teachers arbitrarily to prescribe what experiences children should have, and it is precisely because the centers themselves are open-ended that the framework should be unbending. You must say, "You are going to centers every day and you are going to the centers assigned." Centers used in this way will be utilized to their maximum efficiency and the children will do extremely well. Remember the old self-fulfilling prophecy that people generally rise to the level expected? It works.

I must say, however, that I once had a boy who did not go through the centers. Midway through the second semester, he requested that he be allowed to stay at his seat and I gave him permission. He was experiencing problems at home, was highly nervous, and lacked concentration. I mention this to remind you that in teaching, nothing is absolute and that common sense must prevail. But don't be snookered by the vocal or lazy. Be firm.

3. *Try to have only one person at a center at a time.* The only exception to this rule is the game center, where two children will be working together. This is a most important rule because in this day, solo flights are rare. We are inundated by the group mentality— Little League, Brownies, Boy Scouts—and the television with its constant blare. Many people, including children, do not know how to spend time noiselessly and alone. When a single child is being challenged with a real problem at a center, feelings of self-worth and pride are implanted. From a teacher's viewpoint, this means your classroom will be quiet and busy, and when your classroom is busy, you can forget about classroom discipline problems. There won't be any.

4. *Choose a specified time period and stick to it.* I chose twenty minutes because it seemed long enough for third graders to complete the jobs detailed in this book without boredom. It also fit into my reading class format, which involved two one-hour sessions each day.

Since I had two reading groups, one group could be at the centers for twenty minutes while the other group met with me. The last twenty minutes in the hour were spent in a study session with students at their desks. If you had three reading groups, the twenty-minute length would still work: twenty minutes with the teacher, twenty minutes at the centers, and twenty minutes for the student to work at his desk. The only difference is that you would be teaching sixty, not forty, minutes. I prefer it my way.

What about the child who does not finish his work at a center? If he has done his best, let him hand it in. If he has not completed the task but wants to finish it, time usually can be found in the day.

5. *Keep the centers homemade.* Don't, with the exception of science lab sheets, put the assignments in the form of worksheets. Children are duped enough, to use a bad pun! Centers automatically command more respect if they do not use canned material. Most commercially-prepared material is saccharine and atrocious. *You can do better.* Let there be no blushing lambs, shy deer or owls wearing specs. Instead, use construction paper or tagboard and draw what is needed yourself. It may not be perfect, but it will be *personal* and even young children intuit the difference. If you do have trouble converting some of the material in this book, use an overhead projector or find what you want from illustrations in a magazine. But whenever possible, do the work yourself. It will be more satisfying for you, better for them—and *you can.*

While I am discussing the physical properties of centers, a word should be mentioned about *where* these centers should be. Since all of the centers are numbered, the number tags should hang in a prominent place in the room. But since many of the tasks are portable, they can be picked up at the center, then carried back to the student's seat. Obviously, a science center where experiments are going on should take place at a specific station in the room. An art project usually takes extra space, also.

Where centers are in specific places, care should be taken to define the space. I hung a couple of wooden blinds to separate centers for privacy; similarly, you could use a "curtain" of styrofoam packing shapes or buttons. There are many devices you can create for practically no money.

Now that the principles have been defined, let us look at the mechanics of the system. This book is based on a thirteen-center plan.

Nine of these centers necessitate teacher-made materials; the other four draw upon materials found in most classrooms.

The nine centers in which you do the preparations are: art, reading, cognition, science, language arts, handwriting, creative writing, work-study and listening. Notice that I have not given any of these centers "cute" names because the centers themselves carry numbers. You could add names if you desire.

The four centers which do not require much effort on your part are the record, pulp, manipulative and game centers. (The game center has two numbers since it requires two people.)

Each center is given a number and each child is given a letter. If your classroom has more than 26 students, use symbols such as squares or triangles in addition to letters. The chart is put up each morning. The child finds his letter and instantly knows which two centers he will be doing that day. For clarity, use a red ink for morning centers, green for afternoon.

The key to this plan is that no student goes to the same center twice in a week except for the game center, which is represented by two numbers.

This does not mean that every student goes to every center each week. Since a school week is five days and the centers are used twice daily, that would add up to ten slots. If you want one person in a center at a time, you will have to put up with this imperfection. In other words, my one group of 14 students going to ten centers a week is destined to miss four slots. If this bothers you, there is an easy solution: juggle around the center numbering system after a month and that will change everyone's track. The chart itself stays the same all year.

The important point to remember is that the number of centers is dependent upon the number of students in your largest group. Since I had fourteen in one group, twelve in another, I *had* to have thirteen centers. (Keep in mind that the game center is represented by two numbers.)

Here is the chart I used. It will work for you, too, if there are no more than fourteen in a group. Otherwise, you will have to make your own, based on this idea.

Center Number	1	2	3	4	5	6	7	8	9	10	11	12	13	14
Mon. a.m.	B M	A S	H Y	L X	G V	W	E P	D N	C R	K Q	F Z	O	J U	I T
Mon. p.m.	C Q	K N	I Z	H S	L X	D U	G W	B M	O	J R	A T	Y	E V	F P
Tues. a.m.	L S	F R	E U	I Z	H W	K V	J Q	C P	A Y	B N	X	M	D T	G O
Tues. p.m.	E P	D O	L V	G U	F R	H Q	T	J Z	B N	A M	I Y	X	K S	C W
Wed. a.m.	K Y	G X	J W	V	Z	I T	H S	L R	F Q	E P	D O	C N	B M	A U
Wed. p.m.	I V	H U	X	K W	J T	G S	F R	E Q	D P	C O	B M	A Z	N	L Y
Thurs. a.m.	Z	J T	F R	E P	I O	C N	B M	A Y	K S	V	L U	H W	G X	D Q
Thurs. p.m.	X	E Y	D S	C R	B N	A P	K O	W	L Z	G U	H V	I T	F Q	J M
Fri. a.m.	H U	B M	K O	A N	C P	R	I Z	G V	J W	F T	E S	D Q	L Y	X
Fri. p.m.	A N	Z	B M	O	K S	E Y	D V	F T	G X	L W	C Q	J U	I P	H R

Notes:

Each time period (Mon. a.m., for example) contains two lines, representing the two groups of students.

There are times when a game player is missing a partner. He may then call upon the person at the Pulp Center to play with him.

After the chart is made, cut it apart so that you can place before the children only the daily assignments. The whole chart at once is too much for young eyes to assimilate. Remember to use different colored inks to discriminate between morning and afternoon routings.

Then buy yourself an ordinary kitchen timer. Set it for twenty minutes—one group meets with you while the other group goes to the centers—and watch the system run itself. Reset the timer for the second group and you have a program so self-sufficient that even a substitute teacher can use it. The only time you do the directing is on Monday morning when you take a few minutes to introduce the centers.

Each center which requires paper work must have a collection receptacle. This may be a milk carton, ice cream carton, a folder, whatever. When the student finishes the assignment, he places his work there.

What about the work which builds up at each center every day? First of all, some centers will not have tangible work to assess; and in the centers which do, relax. You will be dealing with the results at the end of the week.

At this point, I must state a pet principle of mine: I do not believe work which has been produced by the student should go unrecognized. I put a mark on *every* piece of work handed in by the student. Therefore, with this system, you will be marking many papers at the end of the week, but I can tell you that it goes amazingly fast. I suspect this is because many of the projects are interesting to read. Also, the checking with this kind of work is not based on a minus-three or a plus-ten because you are dealing with ideas.

You will notice I have designed centers for thirty weeks when the school year is actually thirty-six. Centers should not be used during the first week, probably not the second, or the last. Nor should they be in operation during short weeks such as Thanksgiving, Christmas and Easter. Taking them away at these times provides a textural change and this, too, is good teaching.

Finally, the learning projects which follow were designed for third grade, but most of them would work equally well for older children. Some of the ideas are variations of ideas from other sources; most have been developed exclusively for this learning center system. In all cases, the centers have been tested, modified and improved. Certainly, you will want to make modifications in some cases and I would suggest that you keep a set of notes relating to the effectiveness of each center and to any problems you might encounter.

The projects which follow should make a difference in the *depth* and *scope* of learning which goes on in your classroom. They have worked splendidly for my students and for me. I am happy to share them with you.

Greta Rasmussen
Camano Island, Washington

Centers

Materials: Practice paper, colored paper, pencils, gummed stars or labels. Twine and paper clips for clothesline.

CURSIVE WASH

In the room, you see the alphabet written in cursive. Choose a letter you like and practice writing it in cursive until you think you are good at doing it.

Next, choose one piece of colored paper and, using your pencil, write the letter again—big! When you are happy with its shape, use a magic marker to draw around it so that it stands out. Decorate it with your own colors or markers. Use stickers if you wish.

When you finish, hang your letter on the clothesline.

Directions to students →

Cut shirt shape from colored tag-board. (could also pin instructions to a real shirt) →

Comment:

This beginning cursive activity gives children concrete experience in "playing" with a letter, and starts them thinking in cursive.

The clothesline device is wonderful for displaying all kinds of work. Use twine so that the "clothespins" can be paper clips and string the line across the room. It is a fine mobile bulletin board and children appreciate seeing their work prominently displayed.

DISCOVERING ACIDS

Materials: Baking soda, vinegar, water, lemon juice, tuna can, small spoon for baking soda, paper plates, lab sheet.

Did you know that some acids are poisonous? Did you know that other acids are everyday foods you have tasted before? To find out if these substances are acids, take a small amount of baking soda, put it in the can and then mix one liquid at a time with it. If it is an acid, the baking soda bubbles. Always wash out the can when you are finished and use only a small amount of baking soda each time—please.

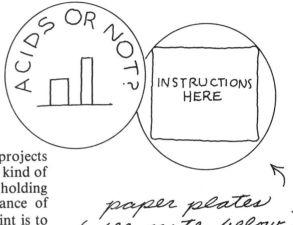

paper plates
(see note below)

Comment:

Children love doing experiments and hands-on projects such as this are marvelous. Since children respect the kind of work going on here, you should not have any trouble holding on to supplies. Be sure to emphasize the importance of answering the last question on the lab sheet. The point is to get them to generalize about what happened.

Experiment No. 1 — Acids Name _____

Directions: Put a check mark in the right box for each item.

	Is an acid	Is not an acid
Example: Pepsi	✓	
Vinegar		
Water		
Lemon juice		

What did you learn? _____

_____

Use paper plates for all science instructions. They are easy and quick to use and will provide your science centers with an instantly identifiable format.

WORD FACES

Materials: Tagboard, felt markers, colored paper, dictionary.

Directions to students →

Each of these faces is telling you a new word. First, look at the word in the mouth and write it on your own paper. Next to the word, answer the question on the face. You need to look up the word in the dictionary to be able to answer the question.

Example: gumbo—Eat it.

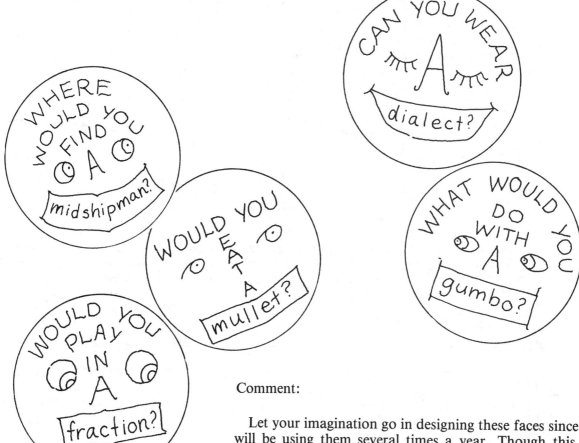

Draw with colored felt markers on Tagboard. ↑

Comment:

Let your imagination go in designing these faces since you will be using them several times a year. Though this is a dictionary project, it goes much further than the usual "write-the-definition" chore by asking the child to process the information once he finds the definition.

The mouth of each face is really an empty rectangle and you tape the word behind it. Therefore, the activity can be easily changed.

Children should be given only one or two of these faces at the first of the year since finding a word in the dictionary can be a lengthy process. Later on, they can work up to all five faces.

Since this is a reusable center, it would be helpful to laminate the faces and spend some time giving the expressions distinction. Notice that the words which make up the questions have been integrated into the design of the face.

BEAN DIP

Children will be spelling with "alphabet" beans so the first order of business is a trip to the grocery store for lima beans. Since you will be printing letters on them, get the largest beans you can find and resist cooking the leftovers—they'll be needed later.

Using several pens with various permanent ink colors, begin printing on the beans (both sides). You will want all the alphabet letters represented; but of course, there should be many more A's than X's. Twenty beans of each vowel should suffice and about that many of the commonly used consonants such as R's and T's. Use only capital letters. Draw a line under letters such as N's and Z's which are easily confused.

Next, cover a coffee can with attractive paper and, if possible, pad the inside with foam rubber or felt because metal is noisy! Put your alphabet beans in the can and include a coffee scoop or tablespoon.

Use the following worksheet for Week 1:

Materials: Lima beans, colored inkpens, 1-lb. coffee can, coffee scoop, worksheet.

Name _____

Directions: Find some words! Dipping into the can, measure out two scoops of beans. Spread them out so that you can see them easily. After you have used several beans to spell a word (and written the word on this paper) put the beans back into the can.

1. In two scoops, I made _____ three-letter words. They were:

_____

_____

2. In two other scoops, I made _____ four-letter words. They were:

_____

_____

3. In two other scoops, the longest word I could make was _____

Comment:

Children like working with the beans and will go about this assignment with diligence. In checking the words they have found, there invariably will be some misspellings at the first of the year. Do not check them wrong; rather, draw a line through them and credit the words which are right. A few children will want to double-check their spellings with the dictionary. Let them.

Materials: Tagboard, felt markers, adding machine tape, cotton balls or marshmallows.

Use cotton balls or marshmallows for word "soft."

THINGS THAT ARE SOFT

On the adding machine tape, make a list of everything you can think of that is *soft*. Be sure to put your name on the back of your list.

Comment:

Hang on to this week's results because you are going to need them at this center next week when the child will begin to classify. From his list of everything soft, he will be asked to come up with things soft and white. In the third week, he will classify those items which are soft, white, and edible.

The adding machine tape is one way to promote fluency. By having the student write his ideas on an unconventional format, such as tape, the assignment encourages associational thinking. Most children like to make lists. Take advantage of this "vertical" impulse.

Materials: Tape recorder, earphones, teacher-made tape, lined paper, pencil with eraser.

You might wish to make a permanent sign for this center.

DO AS I SAY

Through the use of tape recordings, you will provide directions for the children to follow.

When you make tapes, it will save you time if you record several in a session. Have music on hand for the beginning and ending of each recording, since music provides "atmosphere" and a certain professionalism. But please, no Muzak. Be discriminating and give them the best in classical, jazz and contemporary music.

This script takes five minutes, the music three minutes. The student then is instructed to replay the tape to make sure directions have been followed. Care has been taken to allow time for two playings during the twenty minutes.

SCRIPT FOR WEEK 1

(One-minute music) Hello, boys and girls. How are your ears today? We'll find out because this is going to be an experience in listening and in following directions. You are to listen as well as you can and do everything I say. First, take a deep breath. (Pause) No, no, I mean a really big one. (Pause) Okay, you should be ready, and here we go. It should be fun if you listen. You see a stack of lined paper on the desk? Take one sheet and place it before you. (Pause) Now, pick up the pencil. (Pause) Number your paper from one to ten. (Pause) On the first line, write or print your first and last name. (Pause) On line two, scribble all the way across the line. Oh, really scribble—make the lines as dark as you can. (Pause) Next, leave line three blank. Don't do anything to it; don't even breathe on it. On line four, write the name of your very favorite television show. I'll give you a little thinking time. Don't worry about how to spell it; this is a time when I am interested only in your ideas and please, remember, I asked for only one show. If you have two you like the same, you'll have to choose just one for now. (Pause) Oh, oh, I just noticed that the third line—line three—is feeling rather sad because it doesn't have a mark anywhere on it. You must go back now and give it a bunch of zigzags. Will you do this—zigzags for line three? (Pause) On line five, print eight small t's and print three capital m's. (Pause) On line six, draw two squares side by side because they are good friends. (Pause) Oh, now what has happened? The squares are fighting about who stands first in the lunch line. What a silly argument, but they are really mad, so on line seven, draw the two squares again; but this time, put them very far apart, as far apart as you can get them. They aren't even speaking. (Pause) On line eight, write the first word which pops into your mind. (Pause) On line nine, draw three circles and fill them in with dots. They have just come down with the chicken pox and they are feeling quite miserable. (Pause) On line ten, you have quite a job to do. This is where you need to write two words—The End—and write them in such a way that the letters look scared because, frankly, this line is frightened about being The End. Make the words look shaky like my voice is sounding right now: T-T-T-H-E-E-N-D! (Pause) Now you are finished with the exercise. You will have time to push the rewind button and play the tape again. If you find a mistake, go ahead and change it. When you are finished, be sure to place your paper face-down in the tray. Thank you. Good listening and good day. (Two-minute music fade-out)

Comment:

The possibilities are numerous since children love to listen to tapes. At the beginning of the year, teach each student how to run the tape machine, how to rewind the tape, how *not* to touch the "little red button."

When you record, always be sure to pause long enough between directions. You do not want any child to worry about keeping up with your instructions. Especially at first, reassure the child that if a direction is missed, he should go on.

This will be a favored center. They will enjoy it and so will you as listening abilities greatly improve.

WEEK 1   CREATIVE WRITING

Materials: Felt markers, eighteen 5 x 7 note cards, three brass fasteners.

A SHAPE STORY

This project is presented in "book" form. Each "page" is a 5 x 7-inch unlined note card. Use felt markers to create vividly colored shapes and be sure to keep each shape-character the same color throughout.

The first story is provided for the student in order to present the basic concept. The second story is a series of dot representations which the child will interpret on his own paper.

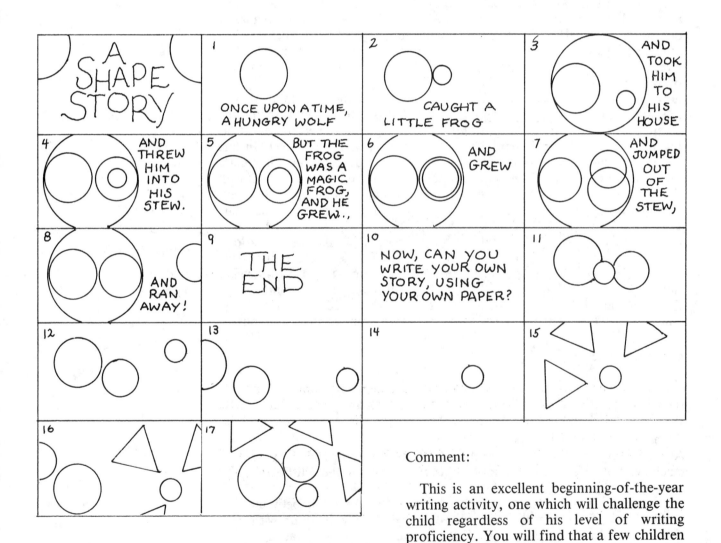

Comment:

This is an excellent beginning-of-the-year writing activity, one which will challenge the child regardless of his level of writing proficiency. You will find that a few children will want to write additional stories, creating their own symbols.

DRAWING THE FAMILY

WEEK 1   ART

Materials: White drawing paper, pencils, crayons, felt markers.

Draw a picture of your family. Be sure to include yourself in the picture. If you have any pets, put them in, too. If you want to show your house, or your living room, that's fine. Put in as many details as you can, and be sure to fill up the whole page.

Your art center should be filled with a changing gallery of art prints by masters. This is especially important for the child whose only encounter with art at home is one bad reproduction centered high and lonely above the family sofa.

We need to help the child become visually astute.

could provide a permanent frame, changing pictures from time to time

Comment:

Most of the art projects in this book have been kept very simple. Materials have been limited to items which are readily obtainable. Most fluid media (tempera, glue, papier-mache, etc.) have been eliminated for obvious housekeeping reasons.

It should be noted that art for children of this age is a very natural process of communication. Children create readily with the knowledge and experience available to them *if* you will allow them to do so. With this in mind, both the projects themselves and the processes involved in their completion place as few obstacles as possible in the way of this natural self-expression.

A word about patterns. You will find no art projects in this book which call for the "manufacture" of identical products such as pinecone turkeys, paper-bag owls or string-art sailboats. Such projects have nothing to do with art, self-expression, growth of self-awareness, and confidence. Avoid them like the plague!

Materials: Cereal box front and side affixed to tagboard.

FOOD FOR THOUGHT

On a separate piece of paper, number from 1 to 8 and write your answers.

1. Who makes Raisin Bran?

2. Raisin Bran is fortified with how many essential vitamins and minerals?

3. Look up the word *essential* and write its meaning.

4. Name five ingredients found in Raisin Bran.

5. How many servings are in this package?

6. Where is Raisin Bran made?

7. How much does this package weigh in ounces (oz.)?

8. What is your favorite cereal and why?

↑ *Directions to students*

Comment:

The point of this exercise is to gain experience in scanning for detail, and cereal boxes have an abundance of factual information. Your project can utilize any kind of cereal, of course, with questions phrased *from the wording on the package.* This is important because children may not know all the words.

Reading all sorts of things stimulates curiosity and learning. The cereal box is a natural. Who hasn't looked at the back of a box while eating breakfast? We are after eclectic readers!

Notice that question three incorporates the dictionary while question eight personalizes the assignment.

PULP CENTER

Bring in some huge pillows, tape together carpet squares for a rug and let them read, read, read. Play to the strength of comic books, popular magazines, even the sports section of the daily newspaper. Let them indulge in free, unfettered reading on their backs, stomachs, sides—no chairs allowed at this center. And keep the informality going by *not* putting the reading material on a bookshelf. A coffee table is better.

For a typical week, I suggest a few of the following:

COMICS	MAGAZINES
Archie	Ranger Rick
Tom and Jerry	World
Richie Rich	Jack and Jill
Superman	Cricket
Classic	Boys' Life
Donald Duck	Children's Playmate
plus	
old comics such as:	
Popeye	
Batman	
Spiderman	

Comment:

Do not make the mistake of putting out too many magazines at once. Eight or ten are plenty. Insist that these magazines stay at the center; they are not to be tucked into desks.

Now and then, include a couple of magazines above their reading level. A Smithsonian or Sports Illustrated would be fine. This is also the place for newspaper clippings which might be of interest.

This center in no way precludes a regular book library in the room. Books should be everywhere.

Note: Since this center does not require further teacher-preparation, it will not appear again in the book.

MANIPULATIVE CENTER

Materials: See below.

Do not underestimate the value of this center even though children may think of it simply as a place to play. It is very important. Not only does it give students manipulative experience, it provides a balance in the overall texture of the program.

This center should be given a specific space in the room. A table, the top of a two-drawer file or a piece of plywood placed on top of an old sewing machine base would be excellent. Ideally, the student should work standing. This provides welcome relief from desk-sitting.

Some of the materials appropriate for this center include:

1. Lego blocks
2. Rubber Parquetry blocks
3. Old typewriter
4. Jigsaw puzzles
5. Lite Brite
6. Geoboard
6. Stamp printing set
8. Magnifying glass
9. Cuisinaire rods
10. Felt board and shapes
11. Playing cards for card houses
12. Calculator
13. Electronic football
14. Magnetic board
15. Dominoes for domino fences
16. United States puzzle
17. Individual slide viewer
18. Constructo-straws

Comment:

This is a popular center as you would expect and it works very well *if* you stick to two rules: Only one child should be at the center at a time and only one activity should be offered each week.

Sometimes a child will not finish a puzzle or a project in twenty minutes. Usually, you can get around this problem by letting the child show what he *has* accomplished. This is only a problem at the first of the year; it doesn't take long for children to become realistic about what they can do.

Don't take this list too literally. You can come up with many other ideas. I happened to buy a big jar of buttons at a garage sale. I brought my button jar to school and used it at this center one week and you should have seen what was done with the buttons! Some children spent the entire time sorting through them, feeling them, experiencing the different colors and shapes. Others classified them into groups. Still others made button houses. The variations were endless.

One tip: Most of the activities will be quieter if you put felt or cloth on the playing surface.

Note: Since this center does not require further teacher-preparation, it will not appear again in the book.

RECORD CENTER

You probably have access to records with accompanying books. Children enjoy reading along in the book as they listen to the story. It is good experience and it provides for a restful interlude in the day.

If you subscribe to any student book club, you know that read-along record sets are readily available.

Hopefully, you can provide the class with a different record every week. If you do not have thirty already in your classroom, borrow from the teacher next door.

This center can be placed next to a reading table or a relatively "active" area since it employs the use of earphones.

GAME CENTER

The games already in the classroom will be fine for this center. There are just two requirements: They have to be games for two players and it should be possible to complete them in twenty minutes.

Games such as these could be used:

Peanut Butter and Jelly
Battleship
Candyland
Checkers
Dominoes
Cards
Junior Scrabble
Game of the States

Do not use educational games—keep this center strictly for fun. Hold your educational games for the regular curriculum.

Do not spend time making games. The commercial games have greater appeal and children already know how to play them. The only exceptions are tic-tac-toe and dot-to-dot (the territorial game where children try to claim squares). These can be made easily and laminated.

Comment:

Stress that games must be played quietly, that tattling will not be tolerated and that everything has to be put away by *both* players when they are finished. This center encourages cooperation, provides practice in playing by the rules and following directions, and offers a pleasant change of pace.

Note: Since these centers do not require further teacher-preparation, they will not appear again in the book.

WEEK 2   HANDWRITING

Materials: Worksheet on colored
stock.

BR-R-R-R-R

Let's Have a Joining Party   Name_____

1. These b's and r's want to be brought together. Bring them together five times IN CURSIVE in the space below.

   br   *br*   *br*   *br*   *br*

2. Now, try these br words in cursive.

   bright   *bring*   *broom*

3. Now, change these words to cursive.

   break
   brook
   brake
   brute
   brrrrrrrrr

4. And write this sentence in cursive: Brushing my teeth is a breeze.

   _____

5. If there is time, turn over this paper and write br as big as you can. Then, in the upper left corner on this side of the page, write it as tiny as you can.

6. Try writing br in cursive with the hand you usually don't use. _____

7. Now, write br in cursive with your regular writing hand and see the difference! _____

Comment:

   There will not be many worksheets in this book, but this is one assignment where the worksheet format works best. The object here is to concentrate on one of the biggest problems in beginning cursive: the joining of the b and the r. Notice that the first part of the lesson requires the student merely to copy the br move, while the latter part asks him to translate the br stroke from manuscript to cursive.

OBSERVING PLANTS

Materials: Two potted plants, magnifying glass, lab sheet, two paper plates.

In front of you are two plants. Pretend you have never seen a plant before. Suddenly, you are seeing every detail. Study the stems, leaves, flowers, shapes, colors, textures, markings. . . everything. Use the magnifying glass to help you. Then, on the lab sheet, write all the ways the plants are alike and different.

When a scientist looks at things very carefully, it is said that he observes. Be a scientist and observe the plants.

Experiment No. 2 -- The Process of Observation   Name _____

Directions: Compare the two plants.

Likenesses	Differences

Comment:

Children are very observant. They find comparisons quite easy to make. This is especially true when you place objects to be compared in front of them.

Choose plants which are markedly different from each other, and turn children loose on their mental dissections.

Materials: Tagboard, construction
paper for picture.

ALPHABETICALLY THINKING. . .

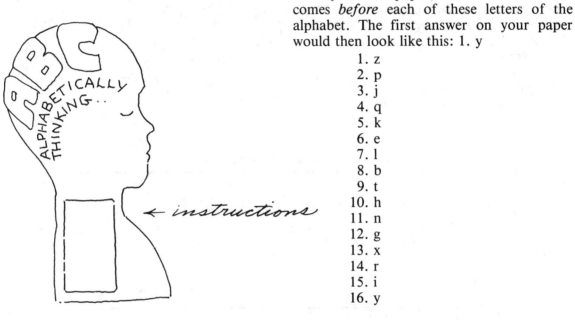

← instructions

Cut shape from
tagboard and
hand-letter.

On your own paper, write the letter which
comes *before* each of these letters of the
alphabet. The first answer on your paper
would then look like this: 1. y

    1. z
    2. p
    3. j
    4. q
    5. k
    6. e
    7. l
    8. b
    9. t
  10. h
  11. n
  12. g
  13. x
  14. r
  15. i
  16. y

If you have time, make a picture using one
of the letters of the alphabet. Here is an
example.

Comment:

Again, you are finishing the experience
with an open-ended task which not only
adjusts itself to the time frame but ends the
work on a high note.

Materials: Dictionary, tagboard.

AUTUMN LEAVES

All of these words have something to do with fall. Read the clues and think! Then write the answers on your own paper. If you can't get an answer, go on to the next clue.

_ _ _ A _ _ _ Light covering for the upper part of your body.

In autumn, the trees _ U _ _ to red and yellow.

_ _ _ T _ _ _ _ Popular game played with a ball.

_ U _ _ Squirrels store these away.

M _ _ _ _ _ _ What birds do in the fall.

_ _ _ N _ _ Autumn color which combines red and yellow.

Back to _ _ _ _ _ L

The season of trick or _ _ E _ _

_ A _ _ What leaves do in autumn.

_ _ _ V _ _ _ moon.

_ E _ _ _ _ _ _ First fall month.

_ _ _ S _ A whitish covering on windows and grass.

Comment:

The answers are: sweater, turn, football, nuts, migrate, orange, school, treat, fall, harvest, September, frost.

On Monday, you should stress that some of the clues may be difficult, but students should try to get as many words as they can. A dictionary at this center for the week is helpful.

Materials: Tagboard, adding machine tape, student lists from last week.

THINGS SOFT AND WHITE

On the desk is the list of soft words you made last week. Now, working with that list, make a *new* list of words which are soft and *white*. Your new list is going to be a lot shorter, isn't it? Perhaps you can think of other words you didn't think of last week. Try as hard as you can.

Put your new work on adding machine tape just like you did last week. When you finish, paper clip *both* lists together and put them in the basket.

Comment:

You have saved the students' lists from last week. Check each day to determine who will be at this center and provide the appropriate list. The student will also need new adding machine tape for this week.

A STORY

Every other week, a commercially-prepared story tape, or a tape you make by reading a story of your choice, will be used at this center.

Keep in mind that students can record stories for you.

Use such a story this week.

CRAZY SENTENCES

Below, you see several pairs of words. You are to use each pair of words in one long, crazy sentence. If you want to use a different form of the word—such as girls rather than girl—you may.

Example: spider-wash. When I *washed* my hands, I saw that a *spider* was dangling from my pinkie finger and he was very dirty so I washed him, too.

1. pajamas-fire
2. crack-suitcase
3. fat-banana
4. hiccups-mountain
5. robbery-rock
6. purple-earthworm

Comment:

Some students will make absolutely outstanding connections. Emphasize on Monday that you will not accept any sentences which join the two words together limply, such as: mountain, hiccups—The mountain had hiccups.

Directions here. (cut out multi-colored letters or use colored markers to give this some gaiety.)

25

Materials: Ruler or straightedge,
pencil, white paper.

2, 4, 6, 8. . . MAKE A PICTURE THAT IS STRAIGHT

Using the ruler and a pencil, make a picture with only straight lines.
The subject is up to you. It can be just a design if you like. Try to make
your lines as interesting as you can. Some can be really dark. Some can
be light. Some long. Some short. Remember, the only rule is: Play it
straight!

Comment:

Here is a good, open-ended project which asks for creativity within a
structure (the straight-line imperative). The fact that one may operate
creatively within a fairly rigid structure is a good thing to learn. Robert Frost
said, ''Freedom is pulling easy in the harness.''

Materials: Tagboard.

MONKEY BUSINESS

Below is a group of words. Quite a few of them have something to do with monkeys. Write the ones which do on your own paper.

animals	pretty	fleas	brown
ocean	noisy	noisy	smiling
clouds	families	burns	ice cream
fingers	polka dots	skinny	smart
carpet	farms	smelly	bananas
trees	school	hairy	dumb

If there is time, write about what you would do if a monkey knocked at your door.

Comment:

Children should be able to link not only the obvious clues, such as bananas, but also the more subtle associations, such as families.

RIDDLE TIME

Materials: Tagboard.

Where do they take sick horses? On your own paper, write the cursive letter which is different in each line and you will have the answer. Then, write the answer two times more in your best cursive!

If you have time, try writing a riddle of your own. Do a few of the words in cursive. If you can do them all in cursive, that will be very good.

(to the horsepital)

Comment:

When children begin writing in cursive, there often is an ancillary problem: They have trouble *reading* cursive. The central activity addresses itself to this difficulty.

The suggestion that they write a riddle of their own, if time permits, allows them to use their own judgment in deciding how much of the riddle they will write in cursive. At the beginning of the year, children should not be forced to write more than their confidence and ability will permit.

Materials: 12 cloth bags (see below), lab sheet, 2 paper plates.

TOUCH!

Our sense of touch is one of the important ways in which we gather information about the world around us. How good is *your* sense of touch?

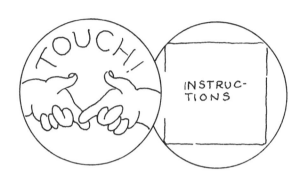

Experiment No. 3—The Sense of Touch   Name _____

Directions: Each bag contains an object you use or should know. Feel the bags carefully. Then record your answers in the squares below.

#1	#2	#3	#4
#5	#6	#7	#8
#9	#10	#11	#12

Which was the hardest bag to guess? _____

Comment:

You will need twelve little bags made out of opaque cloth. It shouldn't take you more than an hour to make them. Drop an object into the bag and sew it competely shut. Remember to keep the objects within the perimeters of young experiences; but do vary them in range of difficulty. Objects might include: a bobby pin, thimble, button, screw, bean, short pencil, earring, ring binder, ring, paper clip, rubber band, acorn, lipstick case, whistle, elbow macaroni, tweezers.

Bags should be labeled by number.

This will be a very popular project.

Materials: Dictionary, tagboard.

ALPHABET ZOO

You have been given an interesting job. You are to start a zoo. But there is one rule you must follow. Your zoo has room for only one animal or bird for each letter in the alphabet. This means your first animal might be an aardvark or an ape, but it can't be both! Use the dictionary and forget about animals which start with x—there aren't any. But there is a bird which starts with a q. Make your list on your own paper.

There are a lot of good display possibilities here — animals made from letters, etc.

Comment:

Some children may not finish this assignment in the required time, but most will want the chance to work on it in their free time. This is a high-interest project; and, while they are enjoying it, they are getting very familiar with the dictionary.

Materials: Tagboard.

WORDWORK

Copy the paragraph below and choose words from the column at the left to fill in the blanks. Make your paragraph funny or serious. Words may be used more than once.

Words to use

vinegar
apple
tooth
flea
tiger
glorp
water
tree
garbage
soda
pear
baby
dog

I was chewing on a_____when I bit into a_____. It surprised me and I yelled to my mother. "Help, help, I need a drink of_____ to wash the _____ down my throat."

"I don't have any_____," my mother said, "so would a drink of_____ be okay instead?"

Comment:

Children love this kind of humor. In the process, you gain a great deal of information about their "ear" for word usage.

Materials: Paper clips, tagboard, worksheet, student lists from last two weeks, adding machine tape.

SOFT, WHITE AND EDIBLE

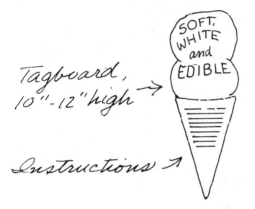

Tagboard, 10"-12" high →

Instructions ↗

In front of you are two lists. The longer one is your list of soft things. The shorter is your list of soft and white things.

This week, you are going to make a third list—of things which are soft, white, and edible. Edible means things you can eat.

Of course, you know that this week's list will be the shortest of all. You'll want to look at last week's list for any items which might fit for this week. Then do more thinking. You might come up with some new ideas.

Put your new list on adding machine tape, too. Then, take the worksheet and fill in the blanks.

Week 1, I made_____words of things which were soft.

Week 2, I made_____words of things soft and white.

Week 3, I made_____ words of things soft, white, and edible.

Edible means _____

The word I like best on my Week 1 list is_____

The word I like best on my Week 2 list is_____

The word I like best on my Week 3 list is_____

The thing I would most like to eat on list 3 is_____

(Clip your worksheet and all three adding machine tapes together and put them in the basket.)

Name_____

Comment:

This beginning classification exercise, which has spanned three weeks, takes the child through the basic steps of classifying material. The worksheet reinforces the concept, since the child is directed to summarize his results.

You can help also by taking a few minutes upon conclusion of this project and listing on the blackboard some of the data which were compiled. On list 3, for example, probably few students thought of cornstarch. Add other ideas of your own, and stress the value of thorough thinking.

MOOD TAPE

Materials: Teacher-made tape, worksheet.

SCRIPT FOR WEEK 3

(One-minute music fade-in) Hello. Today, you are going to be writing some words that help set a mood. If, for instance, you heard this (a door creaking or footsteps) and I said,"Haunted House," could you give me four or five phrases of description that lets me know how you would feel if you were actually going through a haunted house? Close your eyes and while you think about what you are going to write on the worksheet, I'll *really* get you in the mood by providing some more haunted house noises. (If you have a piano, strum the strings inside the piano and you will produce a chilling effect. If a piano is not available, try deep breathing into the microphone, dropping objects, etc. The sound effects should last two or three minutes.) Now, turn off the tape and write words or phrases which would describe your feelings about a haunted house. Do this on the worksheet. (Pause) Next, we have a rainy day. What descriptions could you come up with for a rainy day? (Record drops of water hitting a metal surface. Make thunder by thumping the side of a refrigerator or washing machine. Add other effects, too.) Now, turn off the tape and write some words which describe a rainy day. Think of colors, textures, what you wear, how rain sounds, everything. (Pause) On the worksheet, there are other places and events for you to describe. You may rewind the tape now for the next person to use and then go ahead with your job of selecting words which create a mood. (One-minute music fade-out)

WORDS WITH FEELING   Name_____

A haunted house	A snowstorm	A dog fight
_____	_____	_____
_____	_____	_____
_____	_____	_____
A rainy day	A baseball game	A parade
_____	_____	_____
_____	_____	_____
_____	_____	_____

Comment:

Your tape will not be twenty minutes in length this week because the students need time to finish the worksheet. Your sound effects will be strongly motivational if you make this tape as interesting as you can. This means being a ham, exaggerating, using your imagination.

WEEK 3 CREATIVE WRITING

POWER OF DESCRIPTION

Materials: Rock, tagboard.

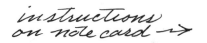
instructions on note card →

Here is a rock. Describe it as well as you can. How many colors do you see? Are there any patterns? Does it feel cold, rough, smooth? What is its shape? What do you like about it? Write every single thing you can think of to say about it on your own paper.

draw a line around your rock

rock

tagboard

Comment:

Needed: one rock. Try to find an interesting rock—something with complexity. You can give this center some presence by drawing around the rock on a piece of tagboard so that the rock will have a place to "sit." Of course, the child should be free to touch, roll, sniff, whatever—short of tossing the rock at someone in the room. An intriguing chunk of wood would work just as well at this center, by the way.

A personal note: I once had a boy who wrote a page and a half of description for this project. Some of the results will delight you.

WEEK 3 ART

BOO!

Materials: Construction paper, paste or tape, scissors.

(This project is early on purpose. Children like living with these characters for a while.)

Are you in a spooky mood? Let's hope so, because your job today is to make a scary Halloween character. Please make your character by cutting and pasting pieces of construction paper together. Try to make your character fairly large. If you make it about as long as the distance between the tips of your fingers and your elbow, that would be fine. You can make a witch, or a cat, or a ghost, or a monster or anything else you like. Just make sure it is scary.

Comment:

This project can yield a fine Halloween-week display for your room or for a hallway. If there is time at the end of the week, you might allow the class to make a Halloween mural made up of all of the characters which have been created. Try not to have any Halloween pictures on display in the room during the week in which this project takes place. As a general rule, it is a good idea *not* to provide visual examples before art projects are produced. Children are copycats.

Materials: Encyclopedia, tagboard.

WHAT ABOUT. . .
PEOPLE IN STRIPED SHIRTS?

1. Get the new Childcraft Book 12, Look and Learn,
   and take it to your desk.

2. Read pages 100 and 101.

3. Answer these questions on your own paper.

   A. If a football referee raises both arms, what does
      it mean?
   B. Describe a referee's shirt.
   C. Why are some signals secret?

If you finish early, read some other articles in this
encyclopedia.

Comment:

Most likely, you have a set of encyclopedias in your room.
Hopefully, they are geared to your children's reading level and are
fairly recent. If the encyclopedias meet these two criteria, use them
frequently in your reading center.

Although questions will be different from those mentioned above,
they should be similar in scope. A few points to remember: be eclectic
in your selections, ask a realistic number of questions, and try to make
the questions interesting.

If you can, include one question which operates on a higher level
(such as question three, which demands deductive thinking).

Do not be too concerned with misspellings and grammatical errors
here. The objective is to see if students have read the article and
understood its meaning.

WEEK 4   HANDWRITING

Materials: White drawing paper, crayons, felt markers.

BREAD TRUCK

Pretend you are the owner of a company that bakes and sells bread. What would your bread truck look like? What would the sign on your truck say?

Draw a big picture of a truck and then, in cursive, write the name of your bread on the side of the truck.

This means that first you have to think of a good name for your bread company!

When you finish, you should have a large picture of a truck and a sign on the side of the truck. The writing on the sign has to be in cursive.

Do not use cursive for this ↗

Do not provide students with a picture of a real truck.

BREAD TRUCK

INSTRUCTIONS

Comment:

Last week, students had to work hard writing the br stroke. This week, they are concerned again with the br move, but in a frivolous way.

Materials: 10 jars (see below), one paper plate, lab sheet.

THEY SMELL

Experiment No. 4 — The Sense of Smell   Name_____

One of our five senses is the sense of smell. How good is yours? In front of you are various jars. Each contains a substance which should be familiar to you. See if you can identify each substance. (Note: Some substances, such as glue, are very dangerous. They should never be smelled for long!)

Jar No. 1 _____

Jar No. 2 _____

Jar No. 3 _____

Jar No. 4 _____

Jar No. 5 _____

Jar No. 6 _____

Jar No. 7 _____

Jar No. 8 _____

Jar No. 9 _____

Jar No. 10_____

Comment:

Use baby-food jars or other uniform containers. Cover or paint the glass so children cannot see inside and poke some holes in the lid to allow the odors to escape. Possibilities: perfume, bouillon cubes, vanilla, almond flavoring, coffee, cinnamon, garlic, parsley, onion, orange juice, lemon juice, vinegar, bubble gum, licorice.

Children will enjoy this week's activity. Be sure to emphasize the dangers of smelling certain substances for a prolonged time.

WEEK 4   WORK-STUDY

Materials: Dictionary. Use Week 1
presentation.

Comment:

Some children will not finish all five
questions. Credit what they do finish.

WEEK 4   LANGUAGE ARTS

Materials: Tagboard.

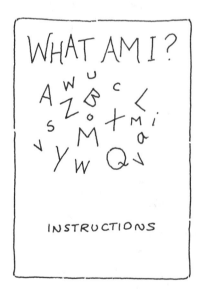

Comment:

The answer is riddle. Number 5
extends the activity for those students
who always finish early.

WORD FACES

Each of these faces is telling you a new word.
First, look at the word in the mouth and write it on
your own paper. Next to the word, answer the
question on the face. You need to look up the word
in the dictionary to be able to answer the question.

Where would you find a mallard?

Can you wear a fez?

Would you play in a mollusk?

What would you do with a peso?

Would you eat a guardian?

WHAT AM I?

Figure out the word, letter by letter. Then
number I-5 and write your answers on your own
paper.

I'm in short but not shot.

I'm in pin but not pan.

I'm in made but not male.

I'm in cold but not cola.

I'm in play but not pay.

I'm in spell but not spill.

1.   What am I?

2.   Write me backwards.

3.   Write me upside down.

4.   Take out my fourth and fifth letters and write
     the word I am now.

5.   Think of other words which will rhyme with
     the word in number 4.

IDEAS THAT ARE ALIKE

Materials: Tagboard.

Below are groups of words which are alike in some way. You must figure out what makes them alike and then add one more word to each set. For instance, meow and hiss would be sounds that a cat makes. To add another word, think of another cat sound. Meow, hiss, purr!

Write the word you add to each group on your own paper.

1. Pennies, nickels, _____

2. Ducks, chickens, _____

3. Table, sofa, _____

4. Eyes, nose, _____

5. Trees, mountains, _____

6. Red, purple, _____

7. Pretty, ugly, _____

8. Bicycle, motorcycle, _____

9. Sled, skis, _____

10. Magazine, comic, _____

11. Hug, pinch, _____

12. Jack in the Beanstalk, Cinderella, _____

13. Snow, ice, _____

14. Henry, Howard, _____

Comment:

There are going to be several assignments in Cognition which promote this kind of thinking. Do not expect everyone to do perfectly the first time. Some children will make the mistake of putting the general category rather than the specific item for the answer. For example, instead of answering *mouth* or *forehead* for number 4, they will write *face*. You will have to determine the grey area in this matter. It is suggested that face might be an acceptable answer for a low-ability child but plainly wrong for a more sophisticated thinker.

A STORY

WEEK 4 LISTENING

Materials: Story tape.

WEEK 4 CREATIVE WRITING

Materials: Three drawings on cards (see below).

WORDS AND PICTURES

Here are three little pictures. Write a short paragraph about what you think is happening in each picture. Do this on your own paper.

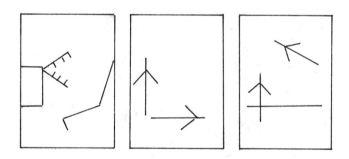

Comment:

Invent your own cryptic drawings if you like. This is a good way to get creative juices flowing. Keeping the drawing on the abstract side increases the creative possibilities.

Materials: Pencils, thin paper such as typing paper, "texture card" (see below).

RUB IT IN!

We use the word "texture" to describe the way something feels. A surface can have a smooth texture, like glass, or a rough texture, like sandpaper. Today, we are going to do some texture experiments. They are called rubbings.

Here's how. Take a piece of paper. Place it on top of the penny. Hold the paper down so it won't move. Now, using the side of your pencil, rub it across the penny. Don't rub too hard, or you'll tear the paper. What happens? If you used enough pressure, you made an image of the penny.

Now, using the same process, place your paper on top of the other objects and make more rubbings. When you finish rubbing the objects at this center, walk around the room and find other textures. Don't disturb anybody.

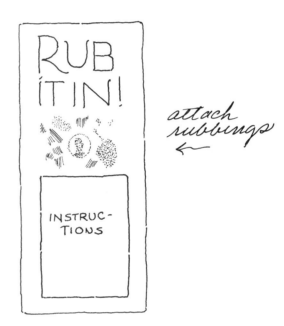

Comment:

This is simply a sensitizing exercise, but children will enjoy it. If you feel a "texture hunt" in the room might be disruptive, suggest that children draw an outline of an animal and use the "texture card" to provide it with fur.

To make the texture card, glue the following to rectangular tagboard: sandpaper, a comb, a leaf, screen wire, a piece of wood, a burlap scrap, buttons, etc. Just about any flat object will do.

Materials: Tagboard, basal reader.

WORD HUNT

Using the basal reader, do the following:

1. Find a one-letter word starting with a.

2. Find a two-letter word starting with b.

3. Find a three-letter word starting with c.

4. Find a four-letter word starting with d.

5. Find a five-letter word starting with e.

6. Find a six-letter word starting with f.

7. Find a two-letter word starting with g.

8. Find a three-letter word starting with h.

9. Find a four-letter word starting with i.

10. Find a five-letter word starting with j.

11. Find a six-letter word starting with k.

12. Find a seven-letter word starting with l.

13. Find an eight-letter word starting with m.

Comment:

For some unexplained reason, this project is received warmly by children. They like word hunts, and they're reading in spite of themselves.

Materials: Tagboard, lined paper.

ANOTHER RIDDLE

What did the joke book say to the egg? On your own paper, write the letter which is different in each line and you will have the answer. Then write the answer twice more in cursive.

(The yolks on me.)

If there is time, write me a short note about anything you like. (I'll write back.) Use as much cursive as you can.

Comment:

Children often get in trouble for writing notes during school time. Give this activity respectability by employing it as an extender to projects at the Handwriting Center.

WEEK 5   SCIENCE

Materials: 12 containers, (see below), lab sheet, one paper plate.

HEAR YE!

Experiment No. 5 — Sense of Hearing   Name_____

   How well do we use our sense of hearing? Each container has a matching sound. Shake the containers and try to figure out which have the same sound. When you are finished, you will have six sets of sounds. List your answer in the space below by writing the two numbers of the containers which have the same sound. Do not take off the caps.

Containers ____ and ____

Containers ____ and ____

Containers ____ and ____

Containers ____ and ____

Containers ____ and ____

Containers ____ and ____

   Ideas I have about what might be in the cans (without looking) _____

_____

_____

Comment:

   It is easiest to get 12 prescription containers for a nominal fee from the drugstore. Then fill them with objects which will make distinctive sounds, such as: bells, erasers, marbles, salt, elbow macaroni, buttons, etc. Children invariably want to guess the contents. Though this is not the intent of the project, an informal question to that effect has been included.

WHICH WAY?

Materials: Map of your state, tagboard.

Read the following sentences. Then write north, south, east or west for each answer. Use your own paper.

1. The house is_____ of the tree.

2. The lake is_____of the garage.

3. The bicycle is_____of the car.

4. The lake is_____of the tree.

5. The house is_____of the car.

6. The bicycle is_____of the garage.

7. The garage is_____of the bicycle.

8. The tree is_____of the house.

If you finish early, look at the map of (your state). Find (your town). Now find (name of another town). What roads would you take to get from (your town) to (the other town)?

Comment:

This task sharpens a child's directional ability. Picture symbols are easy. Draw them yourself on tagboard.

The optional map activity brings map-reading into the realm of places they know. You could add other map questions if you desire.

WEEK 5   LANGUAGE ARTS

Materials: Tagboard.

Directions on reverse →

GI-RAFFE

AN-I-MALS

Think of as many animals with one-syllable names as you can and write them under Number 1 on your paper. (Be sure to leave plenty of space under Number 1.)

Next, think of as many two-syllable animal names as you can and write them under Number 2 on your paper.

Finally, put all three-syllable animal names under Number 3.

For extra credit, can you go on with four-syllable words?

Comment:

Some children may want to continue this assignment beyond the 20-minute time period. And they should.

WEEK 5   COGNITION

Materials: Tagboard, drawing paper.

BRAINSPRINKLE

Answers can be short. Thinking must be long! Write on your own paper.

BRAINSPRINKLE *

* a small brainstorm

INSTRUC-TIONS

1. What happens on the Fourth of July?

2. What foods get harder after they are cooked?

3. Why do leaves turn color in the fall?

4. Where does rain go when it falls on the ground?

5. Why do combs have teeth?

If time remains, draw the fanciest comb in the world.

Comment:

Be glad that there are several Brainsprinkles this year. The answers are sometimes educational, occasionally thought-provoking, and always entertaining. There may be times when a student will want a precise explanation to one of the questions. Be prepared.

Materials: Teacher-made tape.

KATIE

SCRIPT FOR WEEK 5

(One-minute music fade-in) Hello. Today, you are going to be giving your ideas about five different problems; so first I want you to number one through five on your paper, leaving a big space after each number. (Pause) Now, let's talk for a minute about a girl named Katie. She is eight years old and has recently gained a new freedom. She gets to cross busy Washington Street by herself. And since she can cross this busy street, she has become extremely helpful to her mother. Because she now gets to go to the grocery store for her mother. The grocery store is across busy Washington Street and two blocks south, which means a three-block walk for Katie. She is happy about getting this new responsibility. A responsibility means having a certain job to do and being counted on to do it. Being dependable is another way to say it. Some of the responsibilities you might have at home could be cleaning your room on Saturdays or taking care of your baby brother. What responsibilities do you have at home these days? Stop the tape and list them beside number one on your paper. (Pause) As a teacher I have many responsibilities, also. I have the responsibility to teach you how to rename in math and how to write cursive. I have a responsibility to correct papers and hand in reports to the principal. You have school responsibilities, also. Think about what they might be. Stop the tape and write some of your school responsibilities beside number two. (Pause) Getting back to Katie. One day, she had six or seven items to buy at the store for her mother. One of the items was bread and instead of buying the bread, she bought the latest issue of a magazine she had been dying to read instead. Besides, she was sure her mother had a little bit of bread at home and if there weren't enough, she would help her mother make muffins, which could substitute for the bread. And Mother would understand because she knew how long she had been waiting for this new magazine. Kids had rights too, hadn't they? When Katie got home with the magazine instead of the bread, what, if you had been Katie's mother, would you have done? Stop the tape and write your reaction beside number three. (Pause) Katie's mother was mad. Katie's punishment was that she lost the privilege of crossing the busy street and she lost the responsibility of shopping for her mother at the store. Do you think Katie's mother handled the situation fairly? Beside number four, don't write just yes or no, write your opinion, too. (Pause) What if I, your teacher, didn't have any responsibilities? I could get up when I wanted. I could throw a dish on the floor after I had used it rather than wash it. I could eat eighteen popsicles if I wished. I could skip school when I felt like it. I could leave my hair uncombed. Would I be happy? What would happen to me and my job? Just think about it. Then think about a world where everyone had no responsibilities. What would that world be like? Write your ideas beside number five. Then rewind the tape for the next person. Oh, uh, I have to leave now. I have a responsibility to get all those English papers checked. Goodbye. (One-minute music fade-out)

Comment:

The listening center is a beautiful place for values-clarification. This is the first of three real-life situations. Don't necessarily make the responses public. Keep this a center which is quite a private exchange of ideas between you and the student. Have students bring their papers directly to your desk.

Using yourself as an example of an irresponsible person strikes most children funny, while getting the message across at the same time.

Materials: Monkey photo, tag-board.

NAME-CALLING

Answer these questions:

1. What would be a good name for a monkey?

2. What would be a good name for a very tiny dog?

3. What would be a good name for a teacher?

4. What would be a good name for a boy who never combs his hair?

5. What would be a good name for a girl who always yawns?

6. What would be a good name for a flea?

7. What is your full name?

8. Why were you given that name?

9. Do you like your name? Why or why not?

Comment:

The circular format is for manipulative fun. Find a good monkey picture for the middle.

Materials: Stiff paper such as construction paper, scissors, cellophane tape.

PAPER CAPER

Think of all the different things you can do with paper. You can fold it. You can tear it. You can roll it into a ball. You can roll it a different way and make a shape like an ice cream cone. You can make a box if you are careful. You can make hoops by cutting strips of paper and joining the ends. By folding and cutting, you can make all kinds of different shapes.

Now here is a tough assignment. Using only paper, scissors and tape, make any kind of animal you like. BUT. . . your animal must stand up, and it must have some kind of hollow body. In other words, it can't be just an animal shape cut out of a single piece of paper. Good luck!

Comment:

This project will produce many creative results and a bit of frustration. This is a fine exercise in problem-solving and a lot of learning will take place as wobbly-legged animals are coaxed into a standing position.

At the beginning of the week, you might provide a very short demonstration in paper folding and joining.

Completed animals can be placed on the windowsill. With a little taping assistance from the teacher, the paper menagerie should survive a week or two.

Make some drawings or make some shapes from paper and glue to display. →

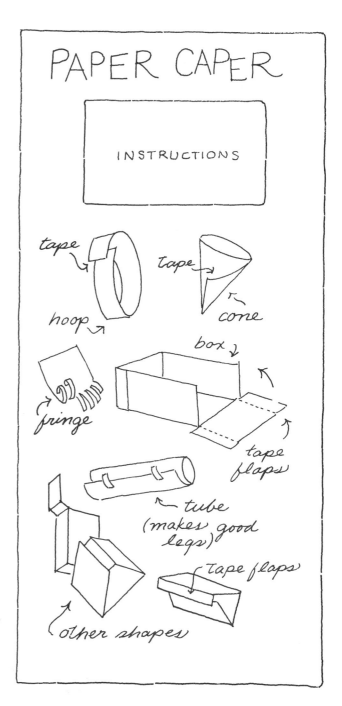

49

Materials: Basal reader. Use Week
4 presentation.

WORD HUNT II

Using the basal reader, do the following:

1. Find a two-letter word starting with n.

2. Find a three-letter word starting with o.

3. Find a four-letter word starting with p.

4. Find a five-letter word starting with q.

5. Find a six-letter word starting with r.

6. Find a seven-letter word starting with s.

7. Find an eight-letter word starting with t.

8. Find a two-letter word starting with u.

9. Find a four-letter word starting with v.

10. Find a six-letter word starting with w.

11. Find any word starting with x.

12. Find a four-letter word starting with y.

13. Find any word starting with z.

If you have time, write the meaning of words
in number 5 and 7.

Comment:

   You might want to display some of these
fourth and fifth-week lists. At the least, share
with the class some of the most unusual
results.

Materials: Tagboard.

LUCKY 7

LUCKY 7 ← write instructions on number.

Spell out the numbers or symbols, put them together, and presto! you have a word. Do all seven on your own paper, and write in cursive.

Example: HIC + 🥣 = HICCUP

1. 10+ T =

2. D+ 1 =

3. 10 + NIS =

4. B + 👂 =

5. C+ 🔒 =

6. 🐀 + T =

7. W+ 8 =

If there is time, write a note in cursive to me, and I will answer it.

Comment:

More thinking than writing is required this week. Since cursive for some youngsters is still a chore, this handwriting assignment attempts to be relatively painless.

Materials: 5 jars (see below), lab
sheet, one paper plate.

MYSTERY POWDERS

Experiment No. 6 — Mystery Powders   Name _____

   Use your senses—*all* of your senses! Try to identify the five powders by feeling, smelling,
looking, even tasting the powders. Record your answers below.

Jar Number 1_____

Jar Number 2_____

Jar Number 3_____

Jar Number 4_____

Jar Number 5_____

Comment:

   This is the last in a series of experiments concerning the
senses, a very appropriate area of investigation for this age.

   Baby-food jars are fine for this experiment. Put the
following white substances in the jars: salt, baking soda,
flour, sugar, and cornstarch. Children may have trouble with
the cornstarch, but some young cooks will know it.

   Warn students on Monday that "taste" means a few grains
on the tip of the finger. Also discuss the idea that they never
taste anything without permission.

   This is a popular experiment.

Materials: White paper, tagboard, ruler.

MAPMAKING

Below are symbols which you are going to use to make a map. You will also need the ruler. Take one sheet of white paper and follow these directions.

1. Place the trees in the middle of your paper.
2. Put the haunted house one inch west of the trees.
3. Put the lake two inches east of the house and one inch north.
4. Make the road run east and west just south of the house and then, when it gets past the trees, have it turn northeast so that it passes on the north end of the lake.
5. After all those directions in Number 4, put the ghosts anywhere you like!
6. The bats are coming in from the west and flying around the trees.
7. Add any other details you wish to make your map complete. You might want to include a church, other roads, some mountains, whatever.

haunted house

ghosts

bats

road

trees

lake

Cut a section from a real map, mount on tagboard, and then mount instruction card.

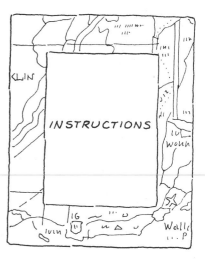

INSTRUCTIONS

Comment:

This is not an easy assignment for some children. Question 4 is intentionally complex. The participatory nature of the project interests all children, however; and the hands-on experience is valuable.

Materials: Tagboard, dictionary.

BLACK CAT COUNTRY

All of these clues have something to do with Halloween. Read the clues, then write the answers on your own paper.

_ H _ _ _   You put on a white sheet and you *are* one.

_ A _ _   Things that fly at night.

_ L _ _ _   cat. (Bad luck to see one on Halloween.)

Go as a _ L _ _ _   with dots for cheeks and a big, sad frown.

_ O _ _ _ _   _ _ _ _   Round, white treat you like to get on Halloween.

W _ _ _ _   A person in a pointy hat.

Trick or _ _ E _ _

_ _ _ _ E   Something worth dunking for.

_ _ _ _ _ _ N   Grows in a big vegetable patch.

INSTRUCTIONS

Comment:

The answers are: ghost, bats, black, clown, popcorn ball, witch, treat, apple, pumpkin.
Some students will need the dictionary handy.

The traditional black cat will do nicely for this.

THE BIORBOSAURUS

I am a new animal. Please don't laugh at me. You may think I look funny, but I am good at doing certain things. Of course, I do have some problems, too. List all of my advantages (good things) and all of my disadvantages (bad things).

Set up your paper this way.

Advantages	Disadvantages

Comment:

Even though the subject is outlandish, children are asked to do some careful analytical thinking.

Directions↑ on back

A STORY

WEEK 6   CREATIVE WRITING

Materials: Clothesbasket full of clothes.

FROM THE SKIN OUT

Make a list of everything people wear on their bodies.

Comment:

The more enterprising may come up with foreign costumes such as kimono and sari.

WEEK 6   ART

Materials: Construction paper, paper fasteners, paper punch, felt markers.

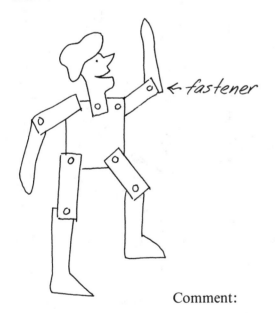

← fastener

Put instructions on a simple card.

ACTION PEOPLE

This week, we're going to make people who can move their arms and legs and head.
Here is what you do.

1. Cut out a body.
2. Make a head. Be sure the head has a neck because you will need the neck to attach the head to the body.
3. Make arms and legs.
4. Use the paper punch to make holes where the arms and legs attach to the body. Be careful not to make the holes too close to the edge of the paper.
5. Join the parts to the body with paper fasteners.
6. Now do the same thing to the head.

Now that your person is all together, use the markers to give him or her a face, clothes and any other details you think of. Take your finished figure to the bulletin board and pin that person in an "action" position!

Comment:

There are directions to be followed here, but the project is flexible enough to allow for plenty of individual expression. The bulletin board display is optional. Figures, posed in active attitudes, could be displayed along a hallway wall or in windows.

Materials: Seventeen 5 x 7 note cards.

THE TRUE AND NOT-SO-TRUE

On the note cards are sentences which are either true or false. On your own paper, number from 1 to 16. Then write true or false beside each number.

1. Pink is really a light form of red.

2. 9987 is less than 9970.

3. In the morning, the sunshine comes from the west.

4. Butter is made by putting cows in cooler places.

5. Wrists are generally smaller than ankles.

6. If you are *reluctant* to do something, it means you really want to do it. (If you don't know the word, look it up!)

7. Airplanes can fly higher than birds.

8. A baseball team is made up of eleven players.

9. Some sharks feed only on people.

10. Television came later than radio.

11. All of the electricity is in the light bulb when you turn on the light.

12. They make plastic from oranges.

13. All four-sided shapes are squares.

14. An ounce is heavier than a pound.

15. February is a winter month.

16. Chefs are required by law to wear tall, white hats.

Comment:

Put each sentence on a 5 x 7 note card. Most children are natural trivia buffs. Take advantage of this interest.

Materials: Tagboard, M & M's.

LET'S HAVE A JOINING PARTY

Lower-case m's can be a pain. Sometimes they look like this _M_ and sometimes they look like this _m_ .

C'mon, _M_ or _m_ , which one are you? Well, it depends on what kind of letter comes *before* an m.

When an a (or any other letter which finishes on the baseline) comes before an m, then an m has three humps, like this _M_ .

When an o (or any other letter which finishes on the midline) comes before an m, then an m has two humps, like this _m_ .

Let's practice.

On your own paper, number from 1 to 10 and follow directions.

1. Copy this: *a small sample*
2. Copy this: *from a zombie*
3. Now, put this into cursive: some shame.
4. And write this sentence in cursive: The smoke gets in the eyes of some champs.

Many words have two m's together. Again, the number of humps depends on the letter before. For instance, you should have six humps for both words in number 5, but the word Tommy in sentence 6 is going to have five humps.

5. Write in cursive: tummy, simmer.
6. Write this sentence: Tommy likes to play.

There are many words which begin with an m. They do fine with three humps.

7. Write in cursive: monkeys misbehaving.
8. Write in cursive: the missing monster.
9. Write this sentence: Mom makes me go to the movies.
10. And, in cursive, write this sentence: Today, we made many m's but the teacher forgot about the best kind of m's and those are M & M's. Maybe she'll pamper us with some this summer.

When you finish, have three on me!

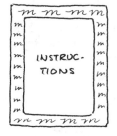

COLORED TAGBOARD

Comment:

Admittedly, this assignment is 99% work and 1% fun (the three-candy hand-out). However, the trouble most children have with the lower-case cursive m clearly indicates the need for a project such as this. And, once they understand the "hump differential," problems cease.

Provide each child at this center with a mere three M & M's. A prejudice of mine is coming out: I do not believe in motivation through bribery; and therefore, tokens should be tokens.

58

Materials: Fourteen 5 x 7 note
cards, plastic dough.

ON THE TRAIL OF TRACKS

Mouse	Rabbit	Squirrel	House Cat	Deer	Raccoon	Opossum
Rat	Dog	Coyote	Fox	Skunk	Beaver	Porcupine

Look at the cards and read the paragraphs below. Then, on your own paper, answer the questions.

After a fresh snowfall, you often can find tracks. The best place to find lots of wildlife tracks is at the edge of the woods or near water. Sometimes, you can see them in your own backyard.

Deer, cats and dogs walk in an almost-straight line. Other animals such as raccoons and opossums waddle as they walk. Since rabbits jump, the back feet land first and leave a long mark. The porcupine leaves a five-toed print that is so large you might think it was a bear!

1. Where are the best places to find tracks?
2. Which animals walk in an almost-straight line?
3. What animal leaves a track which looks bigger than it should, based on his size?
4. Which animals leave four-toed prints?
5. Which animals leave five-toed prints?
6. Which tracks look almost alike?
7. Which tracks look like hands?
8. Which animal leaves the smallest prints?

If there is time, take the plastic dough, smooth it out, and try making some of the prints on the cards.

Comment:

Don't shrink from the drawing part of this assignment. Put one drawing on each card, and keep the images as simple as you see here.

The plastic dough is again a kind of extender for those who finish quickly. Hopefully, most children will get the chance to use it since it provides good, concrete experience.

Materials: Scratch paper, 5 x 7 note
card for finished version, tagboard.

DICTIONARY OF HUMANS!

Rasmussen, Greta (ras′mus un, gre′tuh), n.: 1. She teaches third
grade. 2. She has a husband and two sons. 3. She lives in a big grey
house. 4. She is tall. 5. She likes to read and sew.

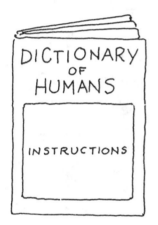

Cut book
shape from
tagboard.

This is a very special dictionary because instead of defining
things, we are going to be defining *ourselves*—and putting us all
together in a class dictionary! Follow my example and do the
following:

1. On scratch paper, write your full name, but put your last name
   first.
2. In parentheses, write your name again, but this time, leave a
   space between syllables and spell your name the way it sounds.
   Also, put an accent mark on the syllable which is said the
   loudest. (Look at the way I have done it.)
3. Put an n. after the parenthesis (as I did). You are a noun, aren't
   you?
4. Next, write down your meanings. In other words, what are the
   most important things about you? Define yourself as I have
   done.
5. When you have finished doing all of the above on scratch paper,
   check any spellings you may not be sure about.
6. Now you are ready to copy your definition on the white card
   for our dictionary.

Comment:

This is a very informal but personalized approach to
understanding the format of dictionary entries. You will
notice that my pronunciation symbols are not "cricket."
This is because my children had not yet had formal study on
pronunciation symbols such as schwas, etc. If your students
have, you will want to change this aspect of the activity.

Children's own definitions of themselves can be extremely
revealing. This is a project which deserves a binding and
cover and public positioning when you have open house.

Materials: Tagboard.

WHO GOOFED?

Read the four sentences. They sound fine when you read them aloud, but they aren't spelled right because some of the words are homonyms. (Homonyms sound the same but may have different spellings.) Write the sentences so each word is spelled properly and use *yore* own paper.

1. Yore dog is board and knowbody nose why.
2. Peal yore pair carefully.
3. Eye can reed and right and eye no that to and to makes for!
4. You weight weather you like it oar knot.

Comment:

Four sentences are enough for students to unravel in twenty minutes. Good spellers will delight in this assignment. Poor spellers may not do as well, but they should get most of the words.

another tagboard shape.

Materials: Tagboard.

LIKENESSES

1. How are ketchup and blood alike? Think of as many *likenesses* as you can. Then do the same with the other pairs of words.
2. Dog-chicken
3. Pencil-spaghetti

Comment:

The more of this kind of thinking children do, the better they get. This is one task where practice pays dividends.

On Monday, emphasize that even though these objects don't *seem* alike at all, there are *many* ways in which they *are* alike.

For number three, children should be able to conclude that both objects are man-made, that they are solids, etc. Number two is purposely easy—once the child thinks anatomically, he is well on his way!

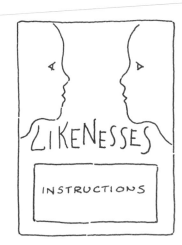

WEEK 7   LISTENING

Materials: Teacher-made tape,
lined paper, pencil.

SAY THE FIRST WORD. . .

SCRIPT FOR WEEK 7

(One-minute music fade-in) Hello, boys and girls. The first direction is to number your paper from one to twenty. Do this now. (Pause) Now, when I say a word, you are to write the first word which pops into your head. Don't worry about whether it has anything to do with the word I said or not. Just put the first word that you think of and don't worry about spelling. Remember, no changes. This is going to be fun. Okay? Here we go. (Pause) Number one. Heavy. (Pause) Number two. Gold. (Pause) Number three. Pup. (Pause) Number four. Black. (Pause) Number five. Funny. (Pause) Number six. Fat. (Pause) Number seven. Thursday. (Pause) Number eight. Thunder. (Pause) Number nine. Kill. (Pause) Number ten. Egg. (Pause) Number eleven. Hurt. (Pause) Number twelve. School. (Pause) Number thirteen. Mean. (Pause) Number fourteen. Good. (Pause) Number fifteen. Face. (Pause) Number sixteen. Play. (Pause) Number seventeen. Small. (Pause) Number eighteen. Fail. (Pause) Number nineteen. Mad. (Pause) Number twenty. Father. (Pause) For the last part of today's assignment, I want you to write a short story using some of the words you just wrote on your paper, BUT this story has to have something to do with a giant. Don't let spelling hang you up, just get busy. Write a wonderful giant story using some of your words. And, any form of the words you wrote will do. If you wrote the word *laugh*, you could use *laughing* in your story. That's all for today. Good-bye. (One-minute music fade-out)

Comment:

Keep your pacing rather fast for the twenty word-associations. Share some of the giant stories with the class later.

WEEK 7 CREATIVE WRITING

Materials: Two sheets of colored construction paper.

POP THE QUESTION

The answers are given. On a separate sheet of paper, you write questions which would fit these answers. Remember, all questions need question marks.

1. I'm eight.
2. I didn't mean to do it.
3. Once every 24 hours.
4. Playing third base.
5. The violin and the piano.
6. I didn't do it.
7. Well, because I felt like it.
8. Everybody else got to do it.
9. It will freeze.

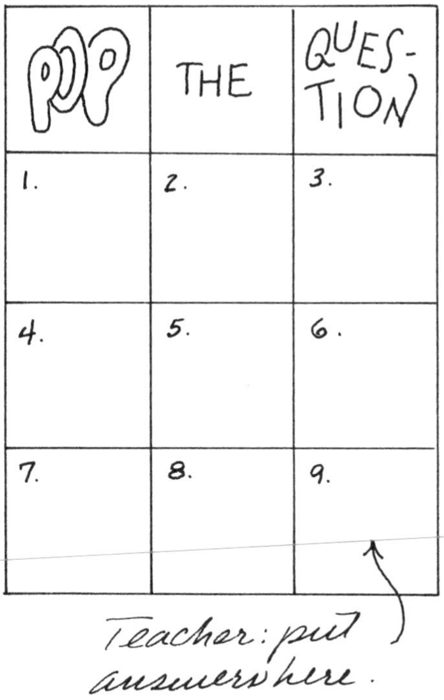

POP
THE
QUES-TION
1.
2.
3.
4.
5.
6.
7.
8.
9.
Teacher: put answers here.

Comment:

There will be three of these assignments, and I suggest that you present them in a similar way. A checkerboard effect is easy to prepare and gives the assignment an inviting look.

Use construction paper, pasting one color onto an 8½ x 11-inch sheet of a different color. It can be accomplished in ten minutes.

WEEK 7   ART

Materials: White-drawing paper,
pencil, crayons, markers.

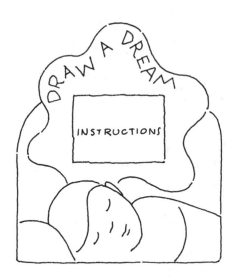

DRAW A DREAM

Think about a dream you have had. Now, using pencil or crayons or markers (or mixing them up if you wish), draw a picture of your dream. If there is time, turn the paper over and write a sentence describing the dream.

Comment:

You needn't be a Freudian scholar to learn a lot about your pupils from this exercise. You might choose to have the children turn in this project directly to you.

WEEK 7   READING

Materials: Tagboard.

BIRDS, BIRDS, BIRDS

Think for a moment about birds. Where do they live? What do they look like? How do they spend their time? Below is a group of words. Many of them have something to do with birds. Write the ones which do on your paper.

If there is time, add a note to your paper telling about birds you have seen in your own yard.

sky	flying
sunburn	buzzing
string	glasses
noses	beaks
trees	watermelon
loud	maple
babies	wheels
dessert	worms
smiling	water
chirping	nests
hair	flutter
roosting	ocean

Comment:

You must be open-minded when assessing these papers. If a child chooses ocean because seagulls live near the ocean, you must give him credit. As you can see, there are only a few words which cannot be associated with birds. No child should be able to talk his way into sunburn as a correct answer!

Materials: Tagboard.

LET'S HAVE A JOINING PARTY N-N-N-NOW!

Lower-case n's can be a pain, just like the m used to be. Because sometimes they look like this _n_ and sometimes they look like this _n_.

C'mon, _n_ or _n_, which one are you? Well, it depends on what kind of letter comes before an n (same as with m—remember?)

When an a (or any other letter which finishes on the baseline) comes before an n, then an n has two humps, like this _n_ .

When an o (or any other letter which finishes on the midline) comes before an n, then an n has one hump, like this _n_ .

Let's practice. Number your paper from 1 to 10.
1. Copy this: *an angry animal*
2. Copy this: *the lone pony*
3. Write this in cursive: Turn the stone.
4. And write this sentence in cursive: The long face of my son pained me.

Many words have two n's together. The first three words you write in number 5 will have four humps each. Poor old Ronnie (the fourth word) will have just three humps.

5. Write in cursive: planner, cunning, funny, Ronnie.
6. Write this sentence in cursive: The winner is Bonnie, who canned the most beans.

There are many words which begin with an n. Just make two regular humps and you'll be fine.

7. Write in cursive: nothing new.
8. Write in cursive: naughty needles.
9. Now write this: Naps are nice if it is not night.
10. And the last sentence in cursive: I knew I needed a nightgown, so I bought one from a nutty clown who fanned himself.

Comment:

Again, a common handwriting problem is targeted. And this time, there are no M&M's at the end of the lesson. If students ask, just tell them you looked but couldn't locate any N&N's for this assignment.

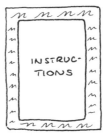

COLORED TAGBOARD

Materials: 10 items (see below),
scale, lab sheet.

LIGHT OR HEAVY

Experiment No. 7—Light or Heavy   Name _____

In front of you are ten items and a scale. Do *not* weigh the items yet. Instead, pick up the objects and guess which one is the lightest, next-to-the-lightest, and so forth, until you get to the heaviest. Write your guesses below.

Then, weigh all the objects and list them from lightest to heaviest, using the scale.

GUESSES	ACTUAL WEIGHTS
1. The lightest item is_____	1. The lightest item is _____
2. Next to the lightest is _____	2. Next to the lightest is _____
3. Then _____	3. Then _____
4. _____	4. _____
5. _____	5. _____
6. _____	6. _____
7. _____	7. _____
8. _____	8. _____
9. _____	9. _____
10. The heaviest object is _____	10. The heaviest object is _____

Comment:

The ten objects can be practically anything you have on hand. If your scale is sensitive, you can include very lightweight objects. However, if you are using a scale which does not register minute differences in weight, your lightest items will be somewhat heavier. It's all relative.

Materials: Encyclopedia, white paper.

FACT AND PICTURE

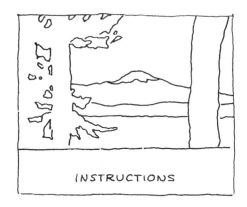

INSTRUCTIONS

Take one encyclopedia from the reference section. Look through it. Find a subject which interests you. Then find a fact about that subject which surprises you.

Make a picture of that fact on one sheet of white paper, and write the fact below it.

Decorate instruction card with an interesting photo.

Comment:

This week, the student decides on the subject for this assignment. Your only involvement should be a warning: once an encyclopedia has been taken, it is kept—no running back and forth to get another one.

Materials: Tagboard "mouth" (see below).

I EAT. . . . Words that rhyme with pie.

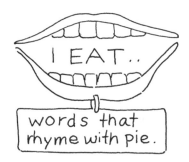

Comment:

Instruct students on Monday to make a list of all words which rhyme with pie. If you feel ambitious, you might wish to cut a slit in the mouth and glue a "drop box" to the reverse side to serve as a receptacle for the lists. Save the mouth, by the way. It will be used several times during the year.

Materials: Purple crayons and markers, tagboard, Week 5 presentation.

BRAINSPRINKLE

1. When the hands of a clock make a straight line (almost) and the small hand is at the twelve, what time is it?
2. Where does wind come from?
3. What is sand made of?
4. Where does wool come from?
5. Orange is made by combining red and yellow. What two colors do you think make purple?
6. Susan walks to Debbie's house. To get there, she passes a park, then a bank, two white houses, a candy store and a skating rink. She takes the same route home. Write on your paper the places she passes in *order* on her way home.

If there is time, turn over your paper and draw a design in shades of purple.

Comment:

The last Brainsprinkle item is a Piagetian-like task to see how well the child does in reverse thinking.

A STORY

WEEK 8 LISTENING

Materials: Story tape.

Materials: One 5 x 7 card.

WHAT DO YOU THINK?

You have a terrible problem. You walked into the dimestore after school and saw your older brother, who is 14, take something without paying for it. It was just a candy bar and the boy he was with took one, too. Your brother didn't see you so he doesn't know that *you* know what he has done.

1. Should you just forget about it? Why or why not?
2. Should you tell your parents? (Sometimes your dad gets very mad at your brother)
3. What should you do?
4. If you took one grape from the grocery store, would that be okay? Why or why not?

Comment:

It is a mistaken notion to assume that creative writing has to come purely from the imagination. Writing assignments which start from realistic premises also call for flexible, creative solutions.

In fact, creative expression cannot be disconnected totally from real experience. It is precisely because of this conviction that most of the creative writing projects in this book may seem quite ordinary. They are designed to start from some familiar reference point for the student, letting him be as creative as he wishes from that point on.

You will notice that students go about these tasks with great enthusiasm and bring forth prolific results, unlike the pie-in-the-sky projects which leave a student saying, "I don't know what you mean."

Think about it.

Materials: Scrap box (see below),
tape, paste, crayons, markers.

Create
a turkey
which
cannot
be copied
by your
students.

GOBBLE GOBBLE

Your job this week is to make a turkey. There is no right or wrong way to make this turkey, because it is supposed to be a funny, imaginary turkey. If you want to make a turkey wearing a hat, that's fine. If you want to give your bird tennis shoes, or a necktie, or even four legs, that's okay, also. The point is, this is supposed to be *your* turkey, so have fun.

You may use any of the materials in the scrap box. Put them together with tape or paste. If you want to use the marker or crayons, do so. Please clean up when you're finished.

Comment:

Collect as many assorted scraps as you can. Old wallpaper samples, fabrics, string, buttons, whatever, will do nicely. Place them in a large cardboard box and have them available at this center.

You may have to do a little explaining to parents accustomed to seeing turkeys made of pinecones, but you can handle it.

I SAY (NOT SIMON). . .

Materials: Colored worksheet, jelly beans, small surprise (see below).

1. Write your first name in manuscript and your last name in cursive.

2. Spell the name of your school backwards.

3. How many words are there in the (name of your local newspaper)? _____

4. Draw a circle and put an x in the middle and give the circle some curls.

5. If you said the answer was ( ) in sentence number 3, go to the teacher's desk and get two jelly beans. If you had another answer, take half a jelly bean.

6. Stand up, pat your stomach and smile at the teacher.

7. If you can get her attention by smiling, go up to her and, without saying anything, shake her hand.

8. If your house is north of (your school), walk around the room two times.

9. If you are wearing blue, go to her desk again and get a jelly bean.

10. If you are wearing anything yellow, go up and get a jelly bean and give it to the person sitting nearest to you.

11. Raise your right hand, touch your nose, and shake your head no for thirty seconds.

12. Write the name of the biggest city in (your state).

13. Go over and pat a wall eight times.

14. If you wrote (name of city) in sentence 12, go write your name on the blackboard.

15. What bird is usually eaten on Thanksgiving? If your answer starts with a *t* and ends with a *y*, go to the basket in the supply closet and get a surprise.

Comment:

Children will think this is great fun, and why shouldn't we all have fun sometimes?

There may be some minor disruptions connected with this activity, but most of the directions call for relatively sedate behavior.

Put this activity in worksheet form as you see here, but do use colored stock.

The "surprise" need not be fancy—a piece of turkey candy or a stick of gum would be quite enough.

There will be similar activities planned for Christmas and Easter vacation. For the few children who would normally not get to this center, be sure to find time for them to get in on the fun.

Materials: Lasagna, tagboard.

WHAT IF. . .

Write small if you can. If you can't, use two pieces of lasagna. →

You have been walking in the woods. You come upon a very special place. It is nice, but when you want to leave, you can't get out. There is nothing to eat in this place—no cows for milk, no berries on the bushes. Then you see a magic button. You press it. Instantly, ten foods appear. You may have to eat them for the rest of your life.

In cursive, list the ten foods you would choose. Remember, you are stuck with these foods *forever*. Think of foods you like but also think of foods which might be good for you.

Comment:

For shock value, try writing your instructions this week on a piece of uncooked lasagna. It works, and fits nicely into the food theme. Then glue the lasagna onto tagboard for strength.

Some children will go about the decision-making process very carefully. You will be surprised at how many practical answers turn up on these papers.

SURFACE TENSION

Materials: Bowl, container of water, measuring cup, small cup, soap, pepper, eyedropper and bottle, paper plate.

Experiment No. 8 — Surface Tension   Name_____

If you watch drops falling from a faucet, you will notice that each drop hangs like a little rubber balloon full of water—until it breaks away.

This water seems to have a tightly-stretched skin. Scientists call this skin *surface tension*. Today, you will be finding out more about surface tension.

1. Fill the bowl with one cup of water. Now, sprinkle some pepper lightly over the water.

What happens?_____

_____

2. Touch the water near one edge of the dish with a wet bar of soap. The moment the bar touches the water, what happens to the pepper?_____

3. Can you figure out what happened to the skin, or surface tension, of the water? _____

_____

4. Now, take the small container and fill it with water to the blue line. With the eyedropper, keep adding drops of water to it. How many drops can you add before it spills? _____

Comment:

Children enjoy this beginning soap-and-pepper activity about surface tension. There is a more ambitious assignment coming up next week on the same subject. It will take a little advance preparation on your part, so be making your plans this week.

The second part of the current project is really an extender for those who may finish early. All that is required is an eyedropper, a bottle filled with water, and a very small container with a line drawn near the top to make the experiment the same for everybody.

You should be prepared to answer basic questions about surface tension. Any science text can help.

Most children of this age, however, are mainly interested in the "doing." Theory can come later.

Materials: Tagboard.

FOLLOWING DIRECTIONS

Line 1: high   get   run   day   month   mother   gopher   house   car

Line 2: tree   sky   earth   yellow   magic   kill   dog   bird   hungry

Line 3: skinny   finger   ring   dress   cool   doughnut   cry   hunt

Line 4: trunk   travel   suitcase   city   store   grass   green   find

Using the words above, follow the directions. Write on your own paper.

1. Write the third word in the fourth line.

2. Write the last word in the first line so that it looks fat.

3. Starting with the first word in line 4, write every other word in that line.

4. A wind blew over the fifth word in line 4. Write it so that the letters lie on their sides.

5. Write the middle word in line 2.

6. Write the second word in line 3 backwards.

7. Write the first two letters of each word in line 1, running them all together.

8. Which lines have the most words?

9. Write the fifth word in line 3 so that it looks as if it is being shouted.

10. Write the third to the last word in every line.

11. If time remains, choose one word from each line and use them together in the best sentence you can make.

Comment:

Following directions is an important part of every school day. It is a skill which can be improved through activities such as this. Give it the attention it deserves.

Materials: Worksheet, dictionary. Use Bean Dip equipment from Week 1.

BEAN DIP

Name_____

Directions: Put the beans back in the can after each instruction. If you need the dictionary to check on a spelling, use it.

1. In one scoop, I made _____ three-letter words. They are:

2. In two scoops, I made _____ four-letter words. They are:

3. In three scoops, I made _____ five-letter words. They are:

4. The longest word I can make in three scoops is _____

5. Spilling all the beans, I can make this sentence:_____
_____
_____
_____

Comment:

The worksheet format is necessary. It structures the activity and directs the learning into small, "digestible" steps.

Materials: Tagboard.

SEEING PATTERNS

Keep the pattern going. Figure out what is happening. Then, on your own paper, continue the pattern by making as many figures as you see blanks. Problem 1, for example, should have two answers.

1. ◯ ⊘ ◯ ⊘ __ __

2. ◯ ◯ ◯ ◯ __ __

3. 1 2 4 5 7 8 __ __

4. AZ BY CX __

5. ▢ I ◯ ▢ I ◯ ▢ I ◯ __ __ __

6. XO XOO XOOO X _____

7. 1 3 5 7 5 3 __

8. ab bc cd de ___

9. 50 100 50 1000 50 _____

10. ◯ ⊖ ⊘ ◯ __ __

11. ⬡ ⬡ ⬡ ⬡ ___ ___

12. Goodbye Goodbye _____

Comment:

Some children cannot get enough of this kind of thinking. Others will have problems with a few of the patterns. Again, however, practice sharpens most children's abilities in seeing relationships and making connections. It is a worthy pursuit.

KEEPING COOL

SCRIPT FOR WEEK 9

(One-minute music fade-in) Hello, boys and girls. Would you please number your paper from one to ten? Today, we are going to be examining expressions we often use in our everyday speech, but which, when you analyze them closely, really don't mean what they say. Confused? Well, you'll understand better if I use an example. For instance, we often say the phrase *How do you do?* when we meet someone for the first time. Think about that phrase. . . *How do you do?* Do what? We really don't mean *How do you do.* . . your hair or *How do you do.* . . at school or whatever. But *How do you do* is a kind of welcome that is polite to say, isn't it? Now, let's examine some other phrases. Oh, by the way, you must excuse me today. I'm kind of *down in the dumps.* "Whhaaaaaat?" you ask. "Wheeeeere are you, (your name)? You're not *down in the dumps*, you're at school!" But, if I would have said first that I hadn't been feeling very well and had been depressed and *down in the dumps*, would you have had an idea about what that expression means? Write beside number one what your idea is. . . the real meaning of the phrase, *down in the dumps.* (Pause) Now I am going to say some other phrases and use them in sentences. When I pause, you write on your paper what those phrases mean. If you get stuck on any phrase, stop the tape and take more time. Ready? Here we go. Number one was *down in the dumps.* Number two is *hot-headed.* I'll use it in a sentence. She would get along much better with other children if she were not so *hot-headed.* (Pause) Number three. The phrase is *on the ball.* Mrs. (school secretary) knows where everything is; she is really *on the ball.* (Pause) Number four. The phrase is *rip-off.* The movie was a big *rip-off*—there wasn't even any plot. (Pause) Number five. The phrase is *raining cats and dogs.* On the day of our big hike, I looked outside and saw, to my disappointment, that it was *raining cats and dogs.* (Pause) Number six. The phrase is *keep your cool.* The important thing in a big game when you're behind seven points with three minutes left to play is for you to *keep your cool.* (Pause) Number seven. The phrase is *stuck up.* Who does she think she is anyway, she's so *stuck up.* (Pause) Number eight. The phrase is *fly off the handle.* He would be a good player if he didn't *fly off the handle* at the slightest little thing. (Pause) Number nine. *Blew it.* He really *blew it* this time by not studying for the test the night before. (Pause) Number ten. The phrase is *drives me bananas.* Having the phone ring when I'm just ready to leave the house *drives me bananas.* (Pause) That's the end of today's assignment. If you wish to run through the tape again and check your answers, do it now. Good listening and good day. (Two-minute music fade-out)

Comment:

Some of the phrases are already familiar to most youngsters. You might want to start a list of other expressions, with contributions coming from the children themselves.

WEEK 9　CREATIVE WRITING

Materials: Ceiling hook, string, white work gloves.

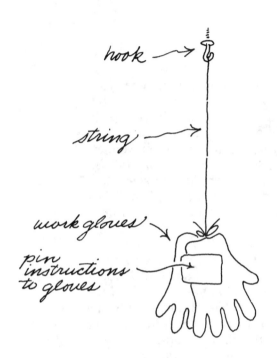

THINGS IN PAIRS

Make a list of everything that comes in pairs.

Make a list of everything that comes in pairs.

Comment:

Put a screw-in hook in the ceiling and hang a sturdy string from it. This device will introduce several of your creative-writing lists this year.

For this week's activity, pin your instructions to a pair of work gloves, and attach to the string.

WEEK 9　ART

Materials: Soft wire (available in hardware stores), small wire cutter (inexpensive and safe).

DOING THE TWIST

Your assignment: Make a wire figure or animal. Start with a long piece of wire from the bag. Twist it any way you can to form the figure. You may use the wire cutter to cut shorter pieces of wire, but it is best to use just one long piece. Good luck and happy twisting.

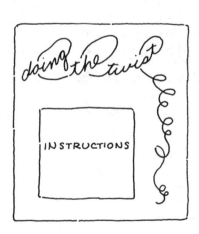

Comment:

This is an excellent sculptural project with very little mess and immediate results. There are good display possibilities, also. Try hanging the figures mobile-fashion.

Materials: Encyclopedia. Use Week 3 presentation.

WHAT ABOUT. . . THE CENTER OF THE EARTH?

A. Get the World and Space Childcraft book.
B. Turn to page 131 and read that page.
C. On a separate sheet of paper, answer these questions as fully as you can (number from 1 to 5).

1. How far is the center of the earth?
2. How far is it to the other side?
3. The outside of the earth is called the _____.
4. Is the middle core hot or cold?
5. Have you ever thought about digging a hole all the way to the other side? What would happen? Have you ever tried?

Comment:

The above questions again relate to a specific assignment and, although your reference books and questions may differ, they should be similar in scope.

Always give children high-interest material to read and questions which are provocative.

All ages should be encouraged to know a little about a lot, and encyclopedias such as Childcraft are filled with riches—yours for the taking.

Materials: Colored construction paper, paste, scissors, black marker.

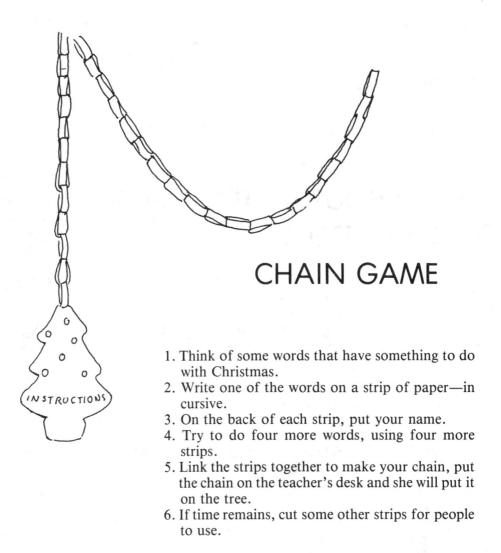

CHAIN GAME

1. Think of some words that have something to do with Christmas.
2. Write one of the words on a strip of paper—in cursive.
3. On the back of each strip, put your name.
4. Try to do four more words, using four more strips.
5. Link the strips together to make your chain, put the chain on the teacher's desk and she will put it on the tree.
6. If time remains, cut some other strips for people to use.

Comment:

This activity is placed early in the Christmas season in order that you may make good decorative use of the chains.

Chains in themselves are busywork; but at this time of year, children love making them.

If you do not have a Christmas tree in your room, festoon the walls. If you do have a tree, put the chains on the tree yourself. Chains are fragile—as are feelings.

Materials: Bubble stand, bubble blower, soap solution, soda straws, wire forms, lab sheet, paper plate.

SURFACE TENSION II — BUBBLES!

Experiment No. 9 — Surface Tension II Name_____

Last week, we discovered that water has a skin which covers its surface. This is called surface tension. Today, we are going to experiment with surface tension again, this time with bubbles. Follow instructions carefully.

1. Dip the wire part of the bubble stand all the way into the soapy water.
2. Then, dip the bubble blower into the soapy water. Take it out and blow a good, big bubble.
3. Put it onto the bubble stand carefully.
4. Take the soda straw and wet it in the soap solution. Then, carefully stick it through the large bubble and try to blow a smaller bubble *inside the large one!*

YOU ARE SEEING SURFACE TENSION AT WORK. . . WHY?

_____

_____

5. Now, take the wire forms and dip them into the soapy water. Do you see the skin, or surface tension, on them when you bring them out? What colors do you see?

_____

Comment:

Bubbles are a natural way to illustrate the principle of surface tension.

Inexpensive soap solution can be made by placing three level tablespoons of soap powder or flakes into four cups of hot water and letting the solution stand for three days. Bubble blowers are readily available in most variety stores.

The bubble stand is easy to make. Glue a dowel about a foot long onto a base. Then wind wire around the dowel and make a loop about two inches in diameter.

Bend soft wire to make the forms. Fashion them into any shape, but do not make the surface area too large.

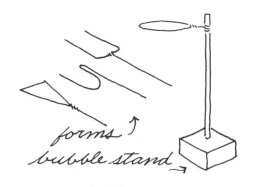

forms ↑
bubble stand ↘

Materials: Guinness Book of World Records, tagboard.

THE OLDEST MARSUPIAL IN THE WORLD. . .

Take the Guinness Book of World Records to your desk and look through it. Make a list of the five most interesting facts you find.

Comment:

Probably the most popular book in the room, the Guinness Book of World Records is simply devoured by children. If you don't have a copy, get one—or two or three.

Again, the assignment attempts to familiarize children with handling reference materials. Having them list the five most interesting facts also helps them organize their thoughts by ordering priorities.

WEEK 10   LANGUAGE ARTS

Materials: Tagboard.

BUILD SOME WORDS

Find as many words as you can by following the lines. No skips allowed, no proper nouns, abbreviations or plurals. Write the words on your own paper.

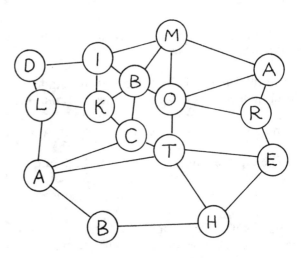

Comment:

You may want to put a similar model on the board and have the class come up with two or three words to show children how to do the assignment.

Materials: Drawing paper, ruler.
Use Week 5 presentation.

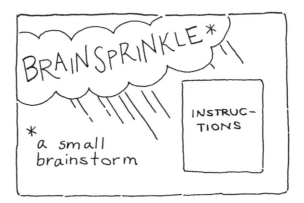

BRAINSPRINKLE

1. What would happen if a dog chewed gum?

2. Where do honeybees go in the winter?

3. What colors have you seen in the sky?

4. How do you know your heart is beating?

5. How long would it take you to walk a mile? Ten miles?

6. Why do things in the distance look small?

If there is time, use one sheet of drawing paper and draw a bunch of things about an inch tall.

Comment:

It is interesting to see how their math holds up in question 5.

A STORY

WEEK 10   LISTENING

Materials: Story tape.

Materials: Tagboard.

LINES DOUBLE NO TROUBLE

On your own paper, think of two lines which could make a rhyme. Here are three examples. See how many you can get.

I like red
but not in bread.

Don't speak to lice.
They aren't nice.

Robins fly
in the sky.

Comment:

Do not expect haiku or cinquain poetry in creative writing projects this year—there won't be any. Poetry of this sort goes against the nature of this age. It is confining, restrictive and overwhelming for *most* children. They dread doing it. Besides, who are we to say that children should be poets? How many adults write poetry or, for that matter, even a descriptive phrase?

However, children at this age love rhymes. Ask them to make up two lines that rhyme and they'll delight in doing it. And, in the process, they may develop a positive attitude toward poetry and a feel for the cadence of language in general.

Materials: Anything! Construction paper, metallic paper, aluminum foil, sequins, paste, tape. (No pinecones or old Christmas cards!)

MERRY CHRISTMAS!

*cut out
Tagboard
shape*

INSTRUCTIONS

Make your own ornament. Use any of the materials you like, but don't make your ornament too big. Try to make an ornament which is really different. It can be something such as a Santa Claus, reindeer, snowflake. . . or it can be just an interesting shape. When you are finished, tie a string on your ornament and hang it on our tree.

Comment:

It should be stressed again that art projects need not be new or original in order to provide a valid creative experience. Your encouragement is all children will need in order to complete this project successfully.

Your class tree may not be beautiful in a "decorator" sense at the end of the week, but, like Charlie Brown's bedraggled little tree, it will have spirit—and that's what counts.

Materials: Tagboard.

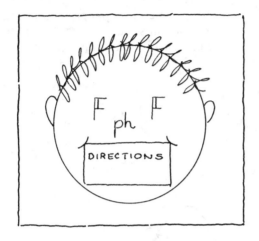

THE F SOUND

There are ten words in this story which have the f sound. Write the words on your own paper. Then do the riddles below the story.

The Story

Jack had to build a fence for his father. But first he had to phone a friend for instructions. When he finished the fence, he was so proud that he took a photograph of it. He didn't know it at the time, but a frog hopped into the picture.

Riddles

What begins with an f and means. . .
1. Second month of the year.
2. Two numbers that add up to nine.
3. A word for the thing you wear rings on.
4. When the river rises and covers the street and goes into houses.

Comment:

In your Monday instructions, emphasize that students are looking for the f sound, not just the words containing the letter f.

Materials: Worksheet, candy.

HIDDEN MESSAGE

Name_____

1. For a secret message, write the first letter where the arrow points and then write every third letter on its right until all the letters are used up. It helps to cross out a letter after you have used it.
2. Now, write the secret message in your best cursive.
3. Do what it says, but keep your actions *secret*.

Comment:

Put this activity on a colored worksheet. It is easier for the student since he can then mark through the letters as he uses them.

The message says, "Go to the teacher's desk for a treat." The treat need not be fancy and should be "hidden" in some sort of a box which says, "For Handwriting Center Students Only!"

WEEK 11   SCIENCE

Materials: 15 rocks (assorted shapes and sizes), two classification cards made of tagboard, 3 x 5 note cards, two paper plates.

ROCKS AND MORE ROCKS

In front of you are two cards. There is also a container of rocks. Working with the rocks, do the following:

1. Group the rocks according to the words on the large card.
2. Group the rocks according to the words on the smaller card.
3. Put the cards aside. Now, put the rocks in order, from the smallest to the largest.
4. Finally, group the rocks a different way and write on a note card how you chose to group them. Be sure to remember to write your name, also.

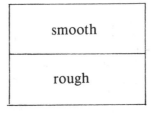

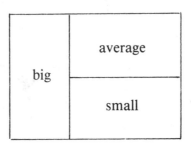

Comment:

The most significant part of this exercise is the note card which will indicate whether the child is able to classify the rocks in another way. Possibilities could include: by color, beauty, shape or weight.

Make both cards large enough to accommodate the rocks.

You will notice that question three is a seriation task.

USING YOUR HEAD

Sometimes, when you are doing your schoolwork, you will have an easier time if you use your common sense.

Below are some questions. On your own paper, write the number which would make the most sense.

1. A classroom is made up of 3, 30, 300 students.
2. The book is 1, 100, 1,000 pages long.
3. A door is 3, 30, 300 inches wide.
4. The man is 6 inches, 6 feet, 6 yards high.
   (Write the number and word).
5. The elephant weighs 2, 200, 2,000 pounds.
6. An eight-year-old boy weighs 9, 90, 900 pounds.
7. The school building is 3, 30, 300 feet high.
8. The school is 1, 1,000, 10,000 years old.
9. (Your name) is 3, 30, 300 years old.
10. There are 6, 60, 600 seconds in every minute.
11. Your hand is 4, 40, 400 inches wide.
12. Your legs are 2, 20, 200 inches long.

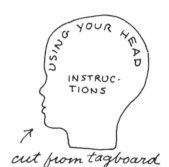

cut from tagboard

And use your common sense to answer these questions:

13. If you had a nail and wanted to hang a picture, which could you use in place of a hammer?
    a. a stick
    b. a brick
    c. a book
14. If you wanted to keep your place in a book but had no bookmark, which of these things would be best to use?
    a. scissors
    b. ruler
    c. cellophane tape
15. If you had to call the police but didn't know the number, (and your parents weren't around) what would you do?

Comment:

Children make a lot of "dumb mistakes" in their school work. Common sense is a teachable commodity—up to a point. Let's teach it.

WEEK 11   LANGUAGE ARTS

Materials: Dictionary, tagboard.

WINTER IS NICE

Think winter! All of these clues have something to do with this cool time of year. Put your answers on your own paper.

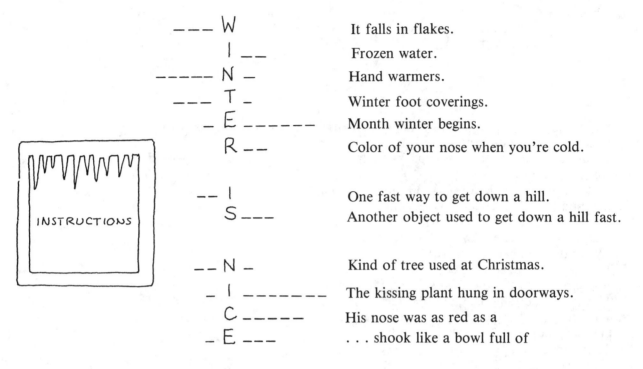

— — — W   It falls in flakes.
I — —   Frozen water.
— — — — — N —   Hand warmers.
— — — T —   Winter foot coverings.
— E — — — — — —   Month winter begins.
R — —   Color of your nose when you're cold.

— — I   One fast way to get down a hill.
S — — —   Another object used to get down a hill fast.

— — N —   Kind of tree used at Christmas.
— I — — — — — —   The kissing plant hung in doorways.
C — — — — —   His nose was as red as a
— E — — —   . . . shook like a bowl full of

Comment:

The answers are: snow, ice, mittens, boots, December, red, ski, sled, pine, mistletoe, cherry, jelly.

Keep a dictionary at this center for the spelling of mistletoe.

WEEK 11   COGNITION

Materials: Instructions taped on plastic drinking glass.

WATER EVERYWHERE

We drink water. But drinking is not the only way we use water. There are many uses for water. List as many as you can. Then go have the world's longest drink of water, compliments of the teacher!

Comment:

Youngsters should be able to do quite well on this assignment. There are many possible answers.

Materials: Teacher-made tape, word beans (see below).

WORD PLAY

SCRIPT FOR WEEK 11

(One-minute music fade-in) Hello. Today, you are going to be using the beans, but these aren't the beans you've used before. Instead of letters, these beans have words on them. Stop the tape right now for a few minutes and look through the beans so that you will be familiar with them. (Pause) Now, write your name in the top right corner of your paper. Number one through five, making sure you leave five or six lines between each number. (Pause) Ready? Here we go. (Pause) Measure out two scoops of beans and, beside number one, list all the words you have which start with the letter s. When you finish, put the beans back into the can. Stop the tape to do this now. (Pause) Next, measure out three scoops of beans and list any words which could be adjectives, or describing words. Stop the tape and put your words beside number two. (Pause) Now, I want you in one scoop to put all the words which have one syllable beside number three. (Pause) Next, beside number four, measure out three scoops and list all the action words, or verbs, which you find. Remember, stop the tape first. (Pause) Finally, using all of the beans, make a long sentence beside number five. It can be silly, but it *does* have to be a sentence and that means your sentence has to have a subject and a verb. . . and. . . it has to be long. That's all for today. Happy beaning. Good-bye. (Two-minute music fade-out)

Comment:

Use your leftover limas for this activity. The best way is to write ten or twelve sentences and then transfer each word to a bean. Write on both sides. Use the Bean Dip container you have already prepared for Language Arts.

Do not forget to include articles, conjunctions, pronouns and prepositions.

For lively sentences, the following words are suggested, in addition to the above: strong, curvy, lovely, dirty, elbows, killed, like, love, hate, house, climb, bubbles, broke, weak, week, fat, skinny, jump, jumped, spill, spilled, splash, splashed, doughnuts, hair, covers, barked, yesterday, today, wet, soggy, socked, itch, itched, spiders, cook, cooked, careful, pajamas, beautiful, green, sparkling.

WEEK 11   CREATIVE WRITING

Materials: Long strip of paper.

THINGS SQUISHY

use string and hook mentioned earlier.

← instructions

On a
separate
piece of paper,
make a list
of squishy things
or make up
a squishy recipe
or do both!

Comment:

Youngsters have a choice this week. Use your string-from-the-ceiling hook-up for this presentation.

WEEK 11   ART

Materials: Bulletin board covered with white paper on which outline of three hills is drawn. Colored markers.

THE THREE HILLS

Using the felt markers, go over to the bulletin board and make some things happening on those three big hills.

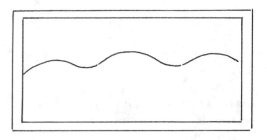

cover bulletin board with white paper, suggest three hills with markers, and stand back!

Comment:

Your answer to the inevitable question, "What should I draw?" should simply be, "Anything you like." As the week passes, your bulletin board landscape will become more and more complex. You may need to instruct children not to draw too large and not to draw over other drawings.

MERRY CHRISTMAS

Materials: Worksheet on colored stock, candy, raisins, surprise.

1. Write your first name backwards _____

2. Make 10 little words using the letters from your first and last names. _____

_____

3. Give your desk a loving pat and then wave at the teacher.

4. If you are wearing socks with blue on them, tiptoe over to the supply cabinet and get one piece of candy.

5. What is the name of our continent? If you don't know, better go to the reference section and find out. _____

6. If a reindeer with big, brown eyes came to your house and your mother said you could keep it, where would it sleep and what would you feed it? _____

_____

7. If you answered question five correctly by writing the words North America, stand up, turn around three times and tiptoe quietly up to the teacher's desk, open her top middle drawer and get a package of raisins.

8. Name your favorite Christmas song. _____

9. What will you be doing during Christmas vacation? _____

_____

10. Yawn once and then stand up and bow to the person sitting nearest to you.

11. If you can tiptoe around the room two times without laughing or talking, you may go over to the storage cabinet, open the lid of the basket, and receive a special Christmas greeting.

Comment:
This is the second of three special-occasion worksheets. Adapt it to your own needs, but keep it light-hearted and fun.

Most teachers give students a small surprise at Christmas. Question 11 gives you the opportunity to do it at this time. If you do not wish to use this chance, simply substitute candy or fruit.

For those students not on the Reading Center track, you will want to arrange a special time for them to do this activity.

WEEK 12   HANDWRITING

Materials: Tagboard.

PARTS OF A CAR

Think of all the parts of a car—inside and out. Write them in a list. Write at least ten of your words in cursive.

Comment:

From a piece of tagboard, fashion a very simple car such as the one pictured. Write the instructions directly on the car.

You will find that youngsters will be full of ideas—and that includes girls as well as boys.

WEEK 12   SCIENCE

Materials: 10 items (see below), container of water, lab sheet, paper plate.

SINK OR SWIM

Experiment No. 10 — Sink or Swim   Name _____

1. Look at the ten objects and guess which ones will sink and which will float on top of the water.

Sink	Float

2. Using the bowl of water, find out if you were right by trying to float the objects.

3. What kinds of things generally sink? _____

4. What kinds of things generally float? _____

5. Do some objects both sink and "swim"? Why? _____

_____

Comment:

The ten items can be practically any small objects you have lying around—a pencil, plastic lid, paper clip, earring, block, toy soldier, eraser, etc. Be sure to include a couple of objects which both float and sink, such as a bottle cap, which floats in an upright position but sinks when turned sideways.

Children will come to realize that trapped air has a great deal to do with "floatability."

CLASS ABC

Materials: Class list (not alphabet-ized), tagboard.

Below are the names of students in our class, but there's one problem. The names need to be alphabet-ized. To do this, you should alphabetize by the last names only. For example, if Betty Bank, Charlie Chew and Bobby Bubble were members of our class, your work would look like this:

> Bank, Betty
> Bubble, Bobby
> Chew, Charlie

Comment:

Alphabetizing is made as palatable as possible because children are working with names they know.

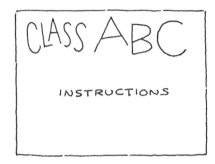

DOGETAR

Materials: Tagboard, adding-machine tape.

Today, you are going to be working with three-letter words first. Here is what you do: I am going to start you working by giving you a three-letter word. Then, you take the *last* letter of that word and make it start your next three-letter word. Keep going and run them all together for one long, long, long word (cross-wise) on the adding machine tape. Do not use the same word twice. Let the example help you.

Example: *dog.* Now I think of a *g* word, *get.* Next, I think of a t word, *tar.* And I put them all together for——*dogetar!*

1. Here's your starting word: *bat*

2. Next, try making four-letter words starting with *pour.*

3. If there is time, do five-letter words starting with *bread.*

Comment:

All children should be able to produce at least twenty three-letter words. Some children will "take wing" on this assignment, compil-ing very wide lists.

Materials: Tagboard.

BRAINSTORMING

1. Think of five scary things. Write them on your paper.
2. Now, circle one of the words you wrote for Number 1. Then make another list of five words which express the circled word.
3. Do this two more times so that you end up with 20 words.
4. If you finish early, express five of the words on your paper in a pencil drawing.

Example: Five weather words—

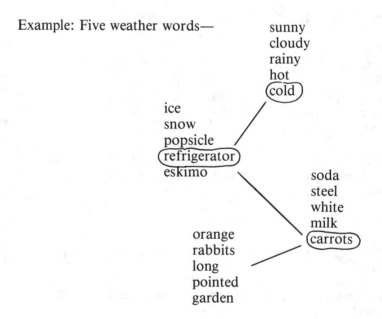

Comment:

Brainstorming produces mental fluency, divergent thinking, powers of association and. . . . entertaining thoughts.

WEEK 12 CREATIVE WRITING

Materials: Instruction card.

WHAT ABOUT

THE PLAYGROUND?

On your own paper, tell what you don't like about the playground. Do this by answering these questions first, then adding any other ideas you have about the playground.

1. Are the rules fair?
2. Should there be other rules?
3. Could the playground be safer?
4. Is there enough to do? If not, what new equipment would you like your school to have?
5. Are there any pieces of equipment which could be made by students for very little money (like a hopscotch court, etc.)?
6. Anything else?

Comment:

It is not too early to encourage critical thinking if it is about something they know. However, children of this age need some direction. "Tell what you don't like about the playground" is not enough. You must take them partway, then let them go.

Materials: Coffee can for water, watercolors, absorbent paper, communal paint shirt.

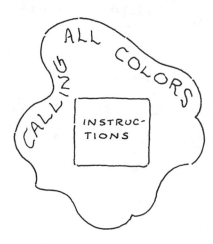

Splash some color on this. Provide a print by Kandinsky, Gorky or some other non-objective painter if you can.

CALLING ALL COLORS

This is your chance to experiment. Can you make a picture that is made up of just shapes and colors? There should be no people or animals or trees or other things we recognize.

Start any way you like. You can make one shape. You can wet the paper and let the colors run together. Or you can paint stripes or squiggles or blobs. Choose colors and shapes you like.

Comment:

What you are asking children to do is to create what is known as a "non-objective" painting (as opposed to an "abstract," where there may still be some recognizable objects). Try to stress the enjoyment which can be derived from interesting color combinations and shape relationships. Do *not* say, "That's very nice, what is it?"

FACT OR OPINION

Some of the sentences you are going to read are facts. Some are opinions. Remember, opinions are what people think or feel. Facts are statements which can be proven. Put an F or O beside each number on your own paper.

1. Winter lasts three months.
2. Last winter, the temperatures were below normal.
3. Winter is my favorite season because I like to ski.
4. Girls shouldn't giggle as much as they do.
5. A frown uses more muscles than a smile.
6. Mrs. (another teacher) is a good teacher.
7. The Rams won the football game 14 to 7 over the Bears.
8. Chuck Hendricks threw the winning pass.
9. Chuck Hendricks is the best quarterback playing the game today.
10. Math is a very hard subject.
11. The sun will set today at 6:22 p.m.
12. Mothballs contain poisons which are dangerous to your health.
13. Spring may come very late this year.
14. Yellow is perhaps a happier color than blue.
15. Orange is a combination of red and yellow.

If time remains, write one opinion about math. Then write one fact about math.

Comment:

Facts and opinions are sometimes difficult for children to distinguish. Curiously, adults have such problems once in a while, too.

Materials: Tagboard.

HAYWIRE SENTENCES

Something is wrong with each of these sentences. Find the mistake, then write the sentences *in cursive* the right way on your paper.

1. Keep off the glass.

2. The ballplayers showed great seamwork.

3. She hopped to get an A on her test.

4. Sometimes, the students try to platter the teacher with apples and flowers.

5. As a result of the accident, one fender was rented.

6. The man and woman were happily marred for thirty years.

Comment:

This handwriting project is designed to be fun. It also gives youngsters an opportunity to practice their cursive.

Children will not get the full import of the sixth sentence, but most teachers should.

BUILD A BOAT

Materials: Aluminum foil, washers, nail, container of water, ruler, paper plates, lab sheet.

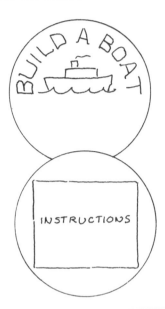

Today, you are going to be a boat builder. Your boat will be made of aluminum. Some real boats are made of aluminum, so you'll be using a good material.

Your boat should be designed for a special purpose: to hold as many washers as possible without sinking. Follow directions and good luck.

1. Using one piece of foil, make your boat.
2. Place your boat in the water.
3. Begin filling the boat with washers. Put the washers into the boat one at a time. . . until it sinks.
4. Take your boat and the washers out of the water and count the washers. Remember the number.
5. Redesign your boat to see if you can make it hold more washers without sinking. Repeat the test, placing washers into the boat one at a time until it sinks. Count the washers again.
6. Fill out the lab sheet.

Experiment No. 11 — Making a Boat   Name_____

1. How many washers did your boat hold the first time? _____
2. How many washers did it hold the second time? _____
3. What did you do to change the boat when you redesigned it?

_____

4. Take a nail and poke a hole in your boat. Place it in the water (without any washers). Does it still float? Why or why not?_____

_____

5. Next, start putting washers in your boat with the hole in it. What happens now?_____

_____

6. How long was your better boat? How wide? Use the ruler to measure._____

Comment:

This project is a logical progression from last week's sink-or-swim activity.

It is important that you provide uniform rectangles of aluminum foil (6'' x 6'' or thereabouts). All washers should be the same size.

Most children will be surprised to learn that the most efficient ''cargo ship'' won't resemble their traditional concept of a boat.

This is an interesting, fascinating challenge for *all* children.

Materials: Dictionary, tagboard.

DICTIONARY GOOSE HUNT

1. Start with the word *elbow*. Look up the word in the dictionary. Write the word *elbow* on your paper and also write the first five words of meaning 1.

2. Now, look up a word which begins with the same letter that the word elbow ends with. What would that letter be? Yes, a *w* word. Write it on your paper and then write the first five words of its meaning.

3. What did your *w* word end with? Find a third word which begins with the last letter in your *w* word and write the first five words of its meaning.

4. Do this again.

5. And once again.
   If time remains, use all five words in a long sentence.

Comment:

Part of the value of this task is in following the directions to the letter.

The reason for asking the students to write the first five words in the meanings is to insure that the work is not carried out solely in the head.

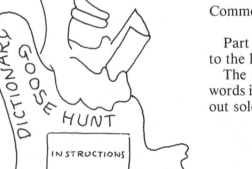

Materials: Tagboard.

ADD AN E

Directions: The first clue gives you one word, then add an e to that word and you should have a *new* word. My example should help you. Please write your answers on your own paper.

Example: Before the present + e = _____ (a sticky substance)

So, the word for the first clue is past. I add an e to past and I should have a word which means a sticky substance. I do! The word is paste!

1. What you do with scissors + e = _____ (good-looking)

2. What your father is, a _____ + e = _____ (neck hair on a horse)

3. Part of a fish _____ + e = _____ (money paid for a speeding ticket)

4. To put your arms around_____ + e = _____ (big)

5. The latest thing, what's "in" _____ + e = _____ (what your tan does in the winter)

6. You burst your button so you need a _____ + e = _____ (evergreen tree)

7. A top will _____ + e = _____ (something that goes down your back)

8. What you take a bath in _____ + e = (toothpaste comes in this)

9. Cleaning "tool" used to wash the floor _____ + e = _____ (acting sad)

10. Baby bear _____ + e = _____ (sugar comes in this form sometimes)

Comment:

Answers are: cute, mane, fine, huge, fade, pine, spine, tube, mope and cube. Most children will not know *mope*; it has been included to make the few who do justifiably pleased.

103

Materials: Use Week 5 presentation.

BRAINSPRINKLE

1. Which is bigger, a mountain or a hill?

2. What is the name of our country?

3. What are drains used for?

4. When you are sick and you close your eyes what do you see?

5. Why shouldn't you scratch a sore?

6. Who invented the light bulb?

If there is time, turn your paper over and draw as many ways of making light as you can.

Comment:

Some of the Brainsprinkle questions are designed to produce in children a *wanting to know* even if they may not always come up with right answers. Many of these questions should be considered "sensitizers." They may not know that Edison invented the light bulb, and they may not have time to find out in twenty minutes, but the question itself starts them thinking.

IT'S IN THE BAG

Materials: Teacher-made tape, walnuts, paper bag, nutcracker, tan box.

SCRIPT FOR WEEK 13

(One-minute music fade-in) Hello, boys and girls. In the paper bag is an object which you will be working with today, but before you open the bag, number your paper from one to five and leave plenty of space between the numbers. Turn off the tape to do your thinking and writing. (Pause) Now, reach into the bag and take out the object. What is it? It is a walnut. Study its color for a moment. What other objects have about the same color? Think of animals, food, plants and other things. Think of *parts* of things. For example, a bread crust is about that color. Put your ideas beside number one. (Pause) Next, pick up the walnut and roll it around in your hand. What does it feel like? Is it smooth, rough, hard, what? Write a sentence or two about how it feels. Do this beside number two. (Pause) As we all know, the walnut has an outer shell. There is a reason for this, of course. The shell protects what is inside. What other things have shells which protect their valuable contents? Think hard. Think of animals with shells, food, everything. Then, write your ideas beside number three. (Pause) Most of you probably have had the experience of taking a pair of pliers or a nutcracker and breaking open a walnut in order to get to the sweet, tasty, delicate nutmeats inside. And just by accident, I happen to have a nutcracker at this center today—it's in the tan box—so, be my guest. Take the walnut, break the shell, but *don't* eat yet. (Pause) Were you lucky enough to get some big pieces when you cracked the walnut? And did you notice how the walnut seemed to be divided into two parts? Examine all the pieces you took out of the shell. Then, beside number four on your paper, draw a picture of your largest and smallest pieces—just the size they really are. (Pause) Finally, I'm going to say it. Your last instruction is to eat. Eat every bit of your walnut—but not the shell, of course. And I almost forgot. There is another thing I want you to do. After you have eaten your walnut, write me a sentence about whether or not you enjoyed your big meal at this center today. Do this beside number five. Good listening, good eating, good-bye. (One-minute music fade-out)

Comment:

Rather than using pliers, which may send nutmeats flying, try to provide a nutcracker.

You will find that some youngsters have a tendency to pulverize the goods. That is their problem, not yours.

Be sure they clean up afterwards.

Materials: Tagboard.

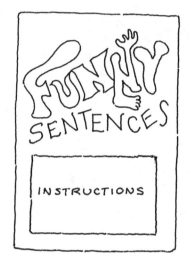

FUNNY SENTENCES

Below, you see groups of three words each. Include the three words in a long, long sentence. If you wish to use a different form of the word, you may.

Example: box, bite, green—I was so hungry that I grabbed the nearest *box* in sight and *bit* into it so hard that *green* gobs of dogs came out.

1. shout, handkerchief, something

2. cover, monster, chin

3. sandwich, noodle, mouse

4. kill, tornado, elephant

5. wall, fry, grasshopper

Comment:

The example is lively to encourage students to be lively, also. Seemingly disparate ideas are fun to link together. Most children can do this very well.

Materials: Paper, brush, black tempera paint, can of water, black felt marker.

MAKING IT SCARY

Take a sheet of paper. Fold it in half lengthwise so that you can find the center line. Then lay the paper flat again. Do the following:

1. On *one side* of the center line, paint swirls or loops or blobs or circles with the black paint.

2. While the paint is still wet, fold the other side over and press down on the paper.

3. What do you see? Go ahead and turn this blob into a monster. Use the marker to give your monster hair, horns, legs, or whatever else you think it needs—and MAKE IT SCARY!

Comment:

Again, this is a simple project which asks the child to put aside the structured behavior necessary during most of the day to do some exploration in his own inner world.

Materials: Yellow page, tagboard.

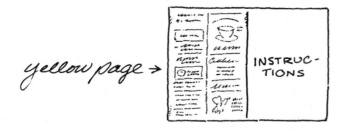

THE YELLOW PAGES

Directions: On a separate piece of paper, number from 1 to 11 and write your answers.

1. The Geode Cafe is in what city?

2. Gabe's Restaurant is closed on _____.

3. If you wanted to phone your order to save time and you were thinking about having a yummy Mamaburger from A & W, what number would you call?

4. Billingsley's Cafe specializes in _____.

5. The first names of those who run the Hi-Hat Cafe are _____ and _____.

6. What is the page number?

7. I need to tell my dad how to get to Hardee's. The street address is _____.

8. There is one restaurant which mentions catfish. Which one?

9. Are you hungry right now? For what foods?

10. If you could go to any restaurant on this page, which one would it be?

11. How many times in a week do you eat restaurant food?

Comment:

Your yellow page will be different, but the questions can be similar. Be sure to select a yellow page which has some display advertising—it produces more varied questions.

Do not worry about the children who do not finish this assignment. Some children are slower than others in scanning for detail.

Materials: Tagboard.

IN PIONEER DAYS. . .

In the early days of this country, pioneers had to figure out how to help themselves when they were sick or had problems. Here are two "recipes" they used.

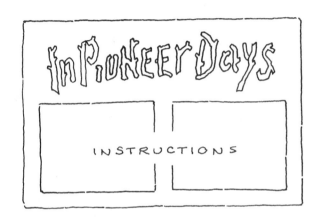

"Really Work 'Em Laxative"

Mix together the following fruit chopped up fine—1 pound prunes, 1 pound raisins, 1 pound figs. Add 1 cup raw bran. Press into shallow pan and cut into squares. Wrap and store in cool place. Take one square daily.

"Toothpaste"

Brush teeth with finely chopped charcoal (wood which has been burned). The best wood to use for charcoal is white ash. A stick end makes a good brush.

Directions: Choose one of the two recipes above and copy it on your own paper in cursive.

P.S. For extra credit, try to figure out the important fact which is missing in the laxative recipe. If you think you know what it is, write it on your paper, also.

Comment:

Again, you are giving children provocative material with which to work. The recipes should be printed, by the way, so that students have the job of transferring the words to cursive.

Incidentally, the laxative recipe doesn't tell how large the squares should be—a rather significant omission.

Materials: 12 unlined note cards, tagboard.

FIGURE RELATIONSHIPS

Spread out the figure cards and group them according to characteristics they have in common. See how many different ways you can group them. Then, on your own paper, write the various ways you grouped them. The example should help you know what to do.

1. One circle only   Figures 4, 6, 9

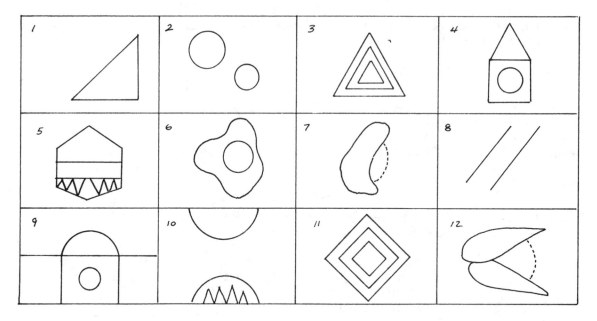

Comment:

This project is a good example of why most of the tasks in this book work for *all* students. A slow student may be doing well to find three ways in which to classify the figures, while a more advanced thinker may classify according to eighteen properties. The important point is: both students are benefiting because the task is valid for both.

Put the figures on individual 5 x 7-inch note cards.

Materials: Local map section, tagboard.

THE MAP

On a separate piece of paper, number 1 to 9 and write your answers based on your reading of the map.

1. The large river which passes through Burlington and Davenport is called the _____.

2. Name three towns which begin with a K.

3. Name the first large town west of Mt. Pleasant on Highway 34.

4. If you were going to Iowa City from Mt. Pleasant, which highway would you take?

5. Ottumwa has a college. What is its name?

6. Beginning at Iowa City, trace the Iowa River southward. Where does it end?

7. The largest city on this map is _____.

8. Spell Mississippi backwards.

9. If you wanted to take a Sunday ride just for fun, where would you go? (It has to be somewhere on this map.)

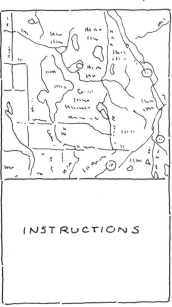

map segment

INSTRUCTIONS

Comment:

It is best to provide a small section of a local map so that the student may deal with locations and names which are already familiar. Some students may not finish and shouldn't be penalized if they try.

Materials: Tagboard.

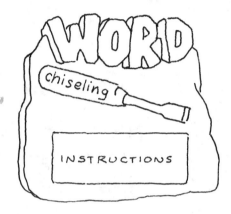

WORD CHISELING

There are lots of words which hide inside big words and all you need to do is "chip" them out. In this exercise, you may not change around the order of the letters, but you can drop letters to find the words.

Example: slicker. Possible little words are lick, lie (dropping the ck), lice (dropping the k)

Your words to work with are:

1. captain

2. information

3. celebrate

4. heavenly

Comment:

There are many possibilities. Keeping the order of the letters—but being able to drop letters at the same time—increases the complexity. Besides, children tire of the assignment which allows letters to be jumbled in any way to make words from one main word.

WEEK 14 COGNITION

Materials: Worksheet.

CATEGORIES

Directions: Fill in as many of the spaces as you can by looking at the top of the column for the topic and to the left for the beginning letter of the word you will be making. Let the example help you. You may not be able to fill in all the boxes, but try!

	BIRDS	STATES	NAMES	CITIES
P	parrot	Pennsylvania		
L				
A				
N				
T				

Comment:

It might be noted again that, although worksheets are generally not used in this learning center system, this is one time when the worksheet device works best. Use colored paper if possible to distinguish it from the mimeographed sea of worksheets used in the regular curriculum.

This particular activity encourages mental agility.

A STORY

WEEK 14 LISTENING

Materials: Story tape.

WEEK 14   CREATIVE WRITING

Materials: "Tall" shape made out of tagboard, ceiling hook and string.

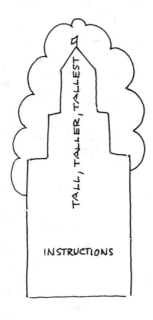

TALL, TALLER, TALLEST

Based on your own size, list twenty things which seem tall to you.

If you have time, guess what is probably the tallest man-made thing in the world. Then guess what is the tallest natural feature in the world.

Comment:

Write your instructions this week on one tall tagboard shape, such as a giraffe or a skyscraper. Hang it from the ceiling.

The answers to the bonus questions are: a radio tower in Poland and Mt. Everest.

WEEK 14   ART

Materials: Paper, pencil

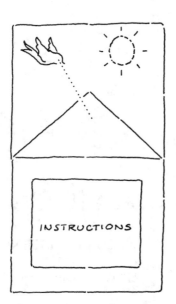

HOUSE DRAWING

If you were a bird and you flew over your house and you could see through the roof, what would you see? Rooms, hallways, tables, chairs, beds, people, dogs, cats?

Make a drawing of how you think your house would look from above if you took the roof off. Include as many details as you can.

Comment:

This task is not quite as easy as it sounds. It requires some conceptual gymnastics in order to keep room arrangements and relationships straight.

Materials: Telephone book, tag-board.

PHONE FUN

See how many names you can come up with for each question by using the telephone book. Examples are in parentheses.

1. List people whose last names are colors. (Dennis Brown)

2. List people whose last names are compound words. (Leslie Shoemaker)

3. List people whose last names are the same as boys' names. (John Randolph)

4. List people whose last names are the same as girls' names. (Sharon Kaye)

5. Find the longest last name you can.

Comment:

Children play informally with names all the time. They develop nicknames for their friends and indulge in puns and word plays. So why not cultivate this fertile ground by utilizing the most obvious name resource of all: the telephone book.

Note that question two is really a language arts application and all questions are making them read—whether they know it or not.

You will want to share publicly the results of this project. The class will be interested in knowing what some of the answers were to question five, for instance.

Hang on to the phone book—you'll be using it twice more. And you might as well make three of the phone shapes out of tagboard now, to take care of the upcoming projects as well as this one.

WEEK 15   HANDWRITING

Materials: Colored paper cut to booklet size, pencil, joke and riddle books, tagboard.

A MILLION LAUGHS

Help! Our class needs a joke and riddle book. Choose one of the jokes or riddles from the magazines and books provided.

In your neatest cursive, write the joke or riddle on one of the colored sheets of paper. Write the answer at the bottom of the page, upside down. If you wish to make a picture along with your writing, you may.

Comment:

Have enough joke and riddle material on hand so there will not be many duplicates when the class book is made.

This is an assignment which promotes class spirit and unity. You might want the class to vote on "class colors" for the cover, which, incidentally, should be designed by the students.

Keep the finished version in a prominent place in the room. By the end of the year, it will look (as it should) very *used*.

WEEK 15   SCIENCE

Materials: String, ruler, line card, one paper plate, lab sheet.

 HOW LONG?

Experiment No. 12 — How Long?   Name_____

Using the string or ruler, measure the lines. Round off your measurement to the nearest inch.

1. _____ inches

2. _____ inches

3. _____ inches

4. _____ inches

5. _____ inches

6. _____ inches

7. _____ inches

8. _____ inches

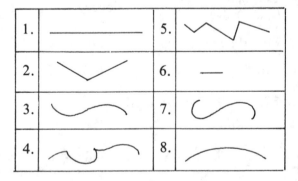

Comment:

Do not make the curved lines too long, or small fingers will have trouble manipulating the string.

When you introduce this center on Monday, do *not* explain that the string is needed for curved lines, the ruler for straight lines. They should discover these things for themselves.

The lines can be drawn with a felt marker on tagboard.

116

Materials: Dictionary, tagboard.

DICTIONARY DETECTIVES

Using the dictionary, follow directions and write on your own paper.

1. Find four compound words and write the page number beside each word.

2. Find a word which has six meanings. Write the word and page where it appears.

3. Can you find a word with more than six meanings? What is it? On what page can it be found?

4. Find and write the longest word you can.

5. Now, write the word in number 4 backwards.

6. Write the first word in the dictionary.

7. Write the last word.

8. Write your favorite word.

9. Write *The End.* Because it is!

Comment:

Somehow this works where out-and-out dictionary assignments do not. Perhaps the reason is that there is an element of mystery here. Students are going on a "search" to locate various data.

Materials: Use Week 4 presentation.

WHAT AM I?

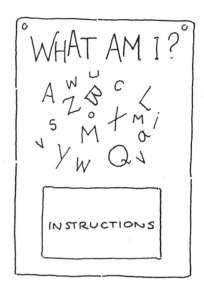

Figure out the word, letter by letter.
Then, number 1 to 4 on your paper.

I'm in cart but not cat.

I'm in bank but not bunk.

I'm in ace but not ate.

I'm in eat but not fat.

I'm in salt but not sale.

I'm in erase but not ease.

I'm in boat but not boot.

I'm in act but not ant.

I'm in kind but not hind.

1. What am I?

2. Which one of these words would describe me?
   Antonym, homonym, compound, synonym,
   verb.

3. Taking the first part of the word, think of
   three other words which would rhyme with it.

4. Taking the last part of the word, use the word
   in a sentence.

Comment:

   The answer is *racetrack*. Questions three
and four test a child's ability to follow
directions while carrying out the actual work

Materials: Use Week 4 presentation.

IDEAS THAT ARE ALIKE

Below are words which are alike in some way. You must figure out what makes them alike and then add one more word to each set. For example, meow and hiss would be sounds that a cat makes. To add another word, think of another sound. Meow, hiss, *purr*.

Write your answers on your own paper.

1. Linoleum, rugs, _____

2. Tulip, rose, _____

3. Pen, chalk, _____

4. Mustache, sideburns, _____

5. Bacon, eggs, _____

6. Tin, iron, _____

7. Rain, snow, _____

8. Skin, fur, _____

9. Square, triangle, _____

10. Ketchup, blood, _____

11. Elbows, hands, _____

12. Bread, doughnuts, _____

Comment:

Use your own judgment regarding how technical you will get when assessing these answers.

The best answers for number five, for example, would be toast, cereal, etc.—thereby classifying by three properties (food, breakfast, solid)—but a slow student who writes pizza and is classifying by just one property (food) is making his own kind of progress.

Materials: Teacher-made tape.

LOUISE AND MARJORIE

SCRIPT FOR WEEK 15

(One-minute music fade-in) Hello, boys and girls. Today, we are going to be thinking about one person who has a problem, and maybe some other people who have problems, too. You'll see what I mean in a minute, I think, but first, number your paper from one to four and leave a big space between the numbers. After each question, turn off the tape and do your writing. (Pause) Now, a word about Louise. She's a girl you might call everybody else's toy because all the kids use her for their play. You see, a lot of kids think she is really ugly. And she wears ugly dresses and she has messy hair. The fun started on the bus one day when Charlie Jones, who just happened to be sitting behind her, touched her and said, "Oh, oh, I've got L-Germs on my hands!" And then he touched Al Smith, and from that day on, everybody made fun by running up to Louise and touching her and bragging about the L-Germs and then running and touching someone else so they could be infected, too. The only person who *didn't* think it was funny *should* have been Louise, but it was someone else. I'll get to that part shortly. As for Louise, she thought it was funny that all the kids were coming up to her like that, and she laughed. Why do you think she laughed? Stop the tape and put your ideas beside number one. (Pause) The game didn't stop. Even at recess, kids would run up to Louise and touch her and then run away. Before too long, Louise would chase after the one who touched her. That was when the game *really* got fun. But the one person who was bothered by all of this teasing was a classmate of Louise's. Her name was Marjorie Hill. She had never teased Louise because she thought it was mean. One day, when the teasing was especially bad out on the playground, she couldn't stand it any longer. She went up to Louise and told her that she didn't like what the other kids were doing and she was going to do something about it. At afternoon recess, she asked Louise to play on the swings with her. Some of the other girls gasped when they saw her playing with Louise and one came up and said, "You'll get L-Germs on you, you'll get L-Germs on you." That did it. Marjorie marched straight to the principal and told on everyone. (Pause) The rest of the week, none of the other children spoke to Marjorie, and Marjorie was very upset. She had tears in her eyes by Friday. Louise came up to her and said, "I'm sorry, Marjorie. Now they don't like you, either." (Pause) Was trying to help someone worth it? Write your ideas beside number two. (Pause) How do you feel about tattling? Everyone in the world has probably done it. When is it all right to tattle? Put your ideas beside number three. (Pause) When shouldn't you tattle? Are there certain times and situations when tattling is wrong? Write your opinions beside number four, then rewind the tape for the next person. And, if you don't rewind the tape, I'll tell on you! Good thinking, good writing and good day. (One-minute music fade-out)

Comment:

This subject matter may cut to the quick, but the presentation is fair. Values-clarification exercises *must* deal with real-life situations, and tattling and teasing are two very real situations in the school environment.

Materials: Tagboard.

TACKLE THIS TASK TODAY

On the table, you see a letter of the alphabet which is going to be *your* letter for this project. This work is going to be divided into two parts.

For the first part today, you are going to write as many words as you can beginning with the sound of your letter. Please include little words, verbs, descriptive words, names, places—every possible word you can think of beginning with your letter sound. You should have a long list. Do not use the dictionary and do not worry now about spellings. The example should help you know what to do.

Example, using the letter o: or, other, ought, otter, orange, orangutan, oh, Oscar, ouch.

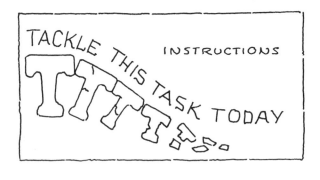

Comment:

The children will not know what the ultimate conclusion of this activity will be. That is fine for now. The important thing is to have them develop long word lists, because next week they'll be writing alliterative stories—using the lists.

If you told a child to write a story using as many s's as possible, he probably would do poorly. If, however, you had him prepare a vocabulary first, he would do much better.

This two-part assignment is very effective. Children will enjoy writing the stories, hearing other stories read aloud, and sharing their stories, also.

You can give several children the same letter—you probably couldn't avoid it anyway—but do not give out letters which would be hard to handle, such as x's, z's, even o's.

You will also want to point out that we are talking not only about letters but also letter sounds. An f assignment would include ph words, such as phone.

When you check these lists at the end of the week, change the words which are misspelled so that children will be working with correct words next week when they write their stories. And, remember to hang on to the lists.

WEEK 15   ART

Materials: Mirror, felt markers, crayons, white paper.

IS THAT ME?

Your job today is to turn yourself into a clown. How? Follow these directions and you'll see.

1. Look into the mirror and, using the black marker, make a drawing of your face. Don't take too long, and don't worry if your drawing doesn't look just like you.
2. Next, pretend you are a clown in a circus and you have to use make-up to put on a clown face. Use the colored markers or crayons to make the drawing of your face into a drawing of a clown's face. You can make it funny, sad, crazy. . . whatever.

Comment:

Again, this is an exercise which promotes creative, flexible thinking. Stress to the children that they need not make accurate self-portraits.

WEEK 15   READING

Materials: Telephone book, tagboard.

PHONE FUN

On a separate piece of paper, see how many names you can find for the following categories. Use the telephone book. Examples are in parentheses.

1. List people whose last names are occupations. (Mary Singer)
2. List people whose last names are animals or flowers. (Bob Rose)
3. List people whose last names are verbs. (James Hatch)
4. List the person whose last name sounds the most important. What do you think he or she might do for a living? What might he or she look like?

Comment:

If the student comes up with the name of Cook for the first category and there are twenty Cooks in the directory, he should know that one name of a kind will suffice.

Be sure to share some of the more interesting finds with the class. This is a fine way to spend a few minutes while waiting for lunch or at the end of the day.

SIX FACTS ABOUT ANIMALS WITH LONG EARS

Materials: Rabbit picture (if available), tagboard.

1. Rabbits are born blind and naked.

2. Rabbits can swim if they are being chased.

3. Many rabbits live in flattened places in the grass. They are called forms.

4. Rabbits are smaller than hares and baby hares have hair when they are born.

5. Rabbits gnaw with their front teeth like rats do, but they are not rodents.

6. Jackrabbits are hares, not rabbits.

In cursive, answer these questions:

1. Where do rabbits live?

2. Name two ways you can tell the difference between rabbits and hares.

3. What do rabbits have in common with rats—even though they are not related?

4. What should a jackrabbit *really* be called?

5. Peter Rabbit was a main character in a famous children's story. He was always getting into a farmer's garden. What was the name of the farmer?

6. A story with a lesson at the end of it is called a fable. One of the most famous fables concerns a race between a hare and what other kind of animal?

SIX FACTS
ABOUT
ANIMALS
WITH LONG
EARS

INSTRUCTIONS

Comment:

Children like facts. They like numbered facts even more. The numbers seem to organize the learning into well-defined "chunks."

This project hardly seems like a handwriting lesson, and that's to its credit. If the material is interesting enough, the cursive will come naturally.

Materials: Snail shell, screw, scissors, paper plates.

SEEN ANY SPIRALS LATELY?

Pick up the shell. Look at it closely. See how it twists and turns upward. It is a *spiral.*

Now, look at the screw. If you look carefully, you will see that it is a spiral, also.

Have you ever seen a spiral staircase? Have you ever thrown a spiral pass in football? Spirals turn and curl. There are some spiders which make spiral webs. Some artists wind material around and around to make spiral baskets.

Today, you are going to make a spiral. Using one paper plate and the scissors, begin at the outer edge of the plate and cut, cut, cut until you reach the center. The thinner you make your cut, the longer your spiral will be! Good luck.

Comment:

This week's science experience is, for the most part, entertainment. Children take great pleasure in making the spirals and in seeing who can make the longest one.

If you don't have a shell, find a picture.

Materials: Construction paper (pre-folded in card format), crayons, markers, tagboard.

WORD-DAY CARD

Using the dictionary, select a word you don't know but which looks as if it might be interesting. Write it on the front of the card. Make it big so that everyone can see that it is a fantastic word.

Next, write the definition of your word on the inside of your card. Put the definition in your own words so that other people in the class will understand it better.

On the back of the card, write the following sentences, supplying the necessary information:

instructions inside

1. My word has _____ syllables.

2. The accent is on the _____ syllable of my word.

3. This is how my word looks backwards:

4. This is how my word looks upside down:

If there is time, decorate your Word-Day Card with crayons and be prepared to send it to someone else in the class.

Comment:

The word-day card serves a two-fold purpose: It acquaints the student with a new word, and it encourages him to apply dictionary skills by examining syllabication, meaning and accent marks.

Kids trade baseball cards, why not word cards? The trading card idea helps personalize the assignment, and the net result is the acquisition of two new words for the vocabulary.

Encourage the students to decorate their cards in preparation for the day when they are "mailed."

WEEK 16   LANGUAGE ARTS

Materials: Use Week 8 presentation.

I EAT. . .

Large, big, heavy words.

Comment:

Use your "mouth" again this week, and be flexible when you judge the answers. *Mountain* would be a good answer since it is certainly large and heavy. Synonyms are more predictable and, therefore, less interesting.

WEEK 16   COGNITION

Materials: Use Week 5 presentation.

BRAINSPRINKLE

On a separate piece of paper, answer these questions:

1. Why is soup put in cans?

2. Why should we cut meat into small pieces before eating it?

3. What is the difference between smoke and fog?

4. Why do married ladies wear rings on their left hands?

5. Who decides where the streets should go?

If time remains, turn over your paper and make a "foggy" picture. Think of how fog makes objects look.

Comment:

Prepare yourself for a variety of replies to question five.

A STORY

WEEK 16 LISTENING

Materials: Story tape.

WEEK 16 CREATIVE WRITING

Materials: Word lists from last week, tagboard.

OSCAR'S ORDER WAS OLD AND ODD

The word list you made last week is in front of you. Pick it up and glance at the words you made. Now you are ready to use as many of the words as you can in a story. You can use other words, too, but try to include as many words as you can with the sound of your letter.

Make it as crazy and fun as you like, but it does have to tell a story. Good luck!

P.S. Remember my "o" list from last week? Well, my "o" story begins this way: Oscar ought to order an ordinary hamburger the next time. This one was old and odd and smelled like oil.

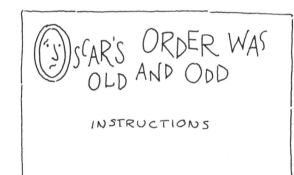

Comment:

Be sure children know that the objective is not to write a tongue twister but an alliterative story. Words which promote the story line cannot always start with the designated letter.

This is one of the best creative-writing assignments. Certain children will achieve incredible rhythmical results.

The alliterative qualities should be exaggerated when stories are read orally. And do not pass up the oral readings—they are fun.

Materials: Medium-sized brown bags, construction paper, string, yarn, cloth scraps, paste, tape.

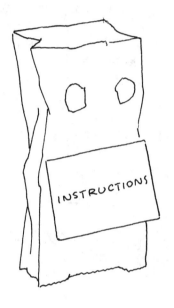

PAPER BAG MASKS

Start with a paper bag. Your job: Turn it into a mask you can wear over your head. Your mask can be anything you like—an animal, a person, someone from outer space. It's *your* mask so you decide what it will be. Make sure you cut out holes for the eyes.

Be sure to throw away the scraps when you're finished.

Comment:

You might plan a five or ten-minute mask show at the end of the week. Masks then can be displayed in a number of ways: hung from the ceiling, taped to a wall, placed in windows, etc. Since visibility in such masks is poor, stress to the children that they should not be worn on the way home.

Materials: Telephone book, tagboard.

PHONE FUN

Find as many names as possible for the following project. Use the telephone directory.

1. List people whose last names are nouns other than occupations. (Jack Penny)

2. List people whose last names have four or fewer letters. (Agnes Lee)

3. List people whose last names are adjectives other than colors. (Paul Swift)

4. List three people who have first and last names with two syllables each. (Robert Raynor)

5. List the name which, if you didn't have your own name, you would choose for yourself. (Do not list friends' names.)

Comment:

This is the final exercise which utilizes the telephone directory. You might wish to do a culminating activity which centers around the fifth question, such as setting aside one hour when students are called by their "wish" names.

WEEK 17 HANDWRITING

Materials: Tagboard.

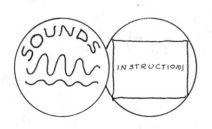

MISSING WORDS

Here are phrases you probably have heard before, but some of the words are missing. Can you come up with the missing words? Use your own paper and write the words in cursive. Write me a note if you finish early.

Example: Nickels and _____. On your own paper, you could write: dimes

1. Ready, set, _____.

2. It's raining cats and _____.

3. Stop, look and _____.

4. Peanut butter and _____.

5. Green eggs and _____.

6. Lions, tigers, and _____.

7. Sisters and _____.

8. Red, white and _____.

9. Boys and _____.

10. Salt and _____.

Comment:

The phrases are not meant to be difficult. They are simply vehicles for the cursive.

WEEK 17 SCIENCE

Materials: Teacher-made tape (see below), lab sheet, two paper plates.

EVERYDAY SOUNDS

In science this week, you are going to listen to a tape. There are a variety of sounds on the tape which you will be asked to identify.

Put your name on the lab sheet first. When you are ready, start the tape and write your answers. You may wish to replay the tape if you run into trouble identifying the sounds. In any event, take a guess at all of the sounds. Every sound is something which should be familiar.

Experiment No. 13—Identifying Sounds   Name_____

Sound 1 _____

Sound 2 _____

Sound 3 _____

Sound 4 _____

Sound 5 _____

Sound 6 _____

Sound 7 _____

Sound 8 _____

Sound 9 _____

Sound 10_____

Below is a series of words which describe various sounds. Try to think of something which could cause each sound.

Example: crash _____. On your paper, you might write: a dish breaking

1. thud _____

2. clatter _____

3. tick _____

4. crunch _____

5. pop _____

6. chirp _____

7. growl _____

8. rustle _____

9. clang _____

10. boom _____

11. whistle _____

12. siren _____

13. rattle _____

14. rumble _____

15. hiss _____

16. bang _____

Comment:

There are many sounds you could record which would be relatively easy, such as: a vacuum, brushing your teeth, blowing your nose, a telephone ringing, a car engine starting, footsteps, your cat meowing or purring, an electric mixer, clearing your throat, a knock on the door, etc. Say the number before each sound so that the student keeps the sounds straight on his lab sheet.

This is simply designed to be an encounter with sounds. You will be dealing with sound more scientifically next week.

Materials: Red and white tagboard, dictionary.

RED!

There are many expressions which begin with the word red. First, look up red in the dictionary and notice all the words which start with red. Then answer these questions. (All underlined words are in the dictionary.)

1. Name one example of a redbird.

2. What is a redbud?

3. What kind of people might be greeted with a red carpet?

4. What is a redcoat?

5. A redhead can be a person with red hair, but it also can be something else. What is it? Look at meaning 2 for the answer.

6. If your business is in the red, or uses a lot of red ink, what is happening?

7. What is a red-letter day?

8. If I say that my job has a lot of red tape, what do I mean?

9. If you get a red ribbon in a contest, do you come in first, second or third?

10. What's black and white and "red" all over? (And not in the dictionary!)

Comment:

Your questions may differ slightly, depending on your dictionary. This assignment is far superior to ten words on the blackboard which the child looks up and defines. There are two more of these "chromo-thematic" activities coming.

Materials: Non-fiction or fiction book, tagboard.

A BOOK LOOK

Using the book provided at this center, follow these instructions.

1. Turn to page 87 and write three nouns in the first paragraph.

2. Turn to page 8 and write three verbs you find on that page.

3. On page 103, write three describing words, or adjectives.

4. Of the sentences in the first paragraph of the book, which seems to be the most important sentence?

5. Find two pronouns on page 78.

Comment:

Any book, non-fiction or fiction, supplies examples of parts of speech, so take advantage of the possibilities. Although this is "bread and butter" work, children immerse themselves in the search.

Materials: Tagboard, white paper
for landscapes.

DROVELS AND SLURPS

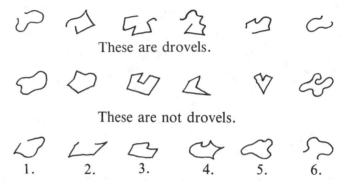

These are drovels.

These are not drovels.

1.   2.   3.   4.   5.   6.

Which of these are drovels? Write the drovels by number on your own paper

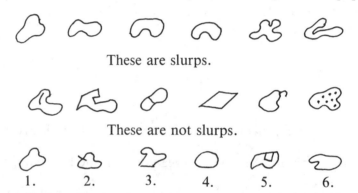

These are slurps.

These are not slurps.

1.   2.   3.   4.   5.   6.

Which of these are slurps? Write the slurps by number on your own paper.

If there is time, make a landscape using slurps and drovels.

Comment:

There will be three of these classification exercises. The first is the easiest
and is designed to give children confidence in identifying the figures
properly.

Drovels are the most elementary, since they are identified by one property
only—their open shape. Slurps are more complex but still readily
distinguishable—they have curved, closed lines and their enclosed space is
blank.

Correct answers for drovels are: 1, 2, 6. For slurps: 1, 4, 6.

Most children will delight in this assignment, but a few may need a little
individual help at first. One or two youngsters may never understand it, but
no matter. This will challenge most of the students and, for the ones who
falter, there is always a slurp-and-drovel landscape to make—even if their
slurps and drovels turn out to be slightly inaccurate.

Materials: Teacher-made tape, crayons, pencil.

FOLLOWING DIRECTIONS

SCRIPT FOR WEEK 17

(One-minute music fade-in) Hello, boys and girls. Today, I want you to number your paper from one to ten, skipping one line between numbers. (Pause) If, in my instructions, I tell you to use a particular color, do what I say. If I do not mention a color, you may assume that I want you to do your work in pencil. Are you ready? Here we go. (Pause) Beside number six, take a blue crayon and draw two squares. (Pause) Beside number ten, draw fifteen x's with a green crayon. When you finish, go back and retrace six of them with a red crayon. This means you will have nine green x's and six red and green x's. (Pause) Beside number three, write your full name in cursive. (Pause) On line one, write the number of people in your family. Remember to include yourself but do not include any pets. (Pause) Write the number of pets you have beside number two on your paper and use an orange crayon, please. (Pause) Still working on the same number, and using a blue crayon this time, write the kind of pets they are. If you do not have any pets, you would just have a zero, wouldn't you, written with the orange crayon. (Pause) Beside number four, write your lucky number. If you don't have a lucky number, leave it blank. (Pause) Beside number five, draw three circles with a purple crayon. Color in the circles with purple, too. (Pause) Beside number seven, draw a line which looks very angry. (Pause) Beside number eight, draw a piece of pie, (Pause) and beside number nine, write what kind of pie you would like it to be. In the time which remains, turn your paper to the other side and, with pencil and crayons, draw a picture which includes four circles, two triangles and one square. But first, you may want to rewind the tape and listen to the directions again. If you find that you have missed a direction, just do that part of the exercise again. Then do your picture. Good listening and good day. (One-minute music fade-out)

Comment:

The directions are intended to be more complicated this time. It should be interesting to see how they handle this level of difficulty. Be sure to speak slowly and pause long enough between directions.

WEEK 17 CREATIVE WRITING

Materials: 3 pictures (see below), tagboard.

THREE PICTURES

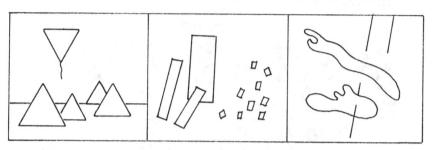

Look at the three pictures. Write a short paragraph telling about what you think is happening in each picture. Really try to use your imagination!

Comment:

Some more abstract art. . . and you shouldn't get too many package replies! It is fun to see how literally they take these drawings.

WEEK 17 ART

Materials: Shoe boxes, construction paper, scissors, paste, tape, pencil, markers.

This is the general idea . . . lots of possibilities!

SHOE-BOX DIORAMAS

Work on one of the three shoe boxes you see here. Use the scissors to cut out shapes of little things you want to put in the shoe-box scene. You can make people, animals, cars, houses, fences, trees—all sorts of things.

Use a marker or pencil to put in the details, and use tape or paste to put your objects in place.

If you want to start working on a different shoe-box scene, you may.

Comment:

This is another of those tried-and-true projects sure to engage youngsters. It would be a good idea for you to prepare two or three shoe-box backgrounds. . . green or brown for ground, blue sky, maybe a cloud or two for an outdoor scene. Perhaps, you also might suggest an indoor environment by simulating a window or door.

Materials: 19 note cards.

THE TRUE AND NOT-SO-TRUE

On the note cards are sentences which are either true or false. Number from 1 to 18 on your own paper, then write true or false for your answers. Feel free to use the encyclopedias or dictionary if you run into a problem.

1. Bears migrate in the winter.

2. When water boils, part of it escapes as steam.

3. A hammer is used basically for joining two things together, but a saw generally separates.

4. All clouds cause rain.

5. Some people must have their crazy bones fixed so that they act more like human beings.

6. Cactus plants usually like sunlight better than other house plants.

7. The longer the root, the stronger the plant.

8. Seeds are often carried by wind and by birds.

9. Owls can turn their heads all the way around.

10. Your mother's sister would be your aunt.

11. Your great-grandfather would be your father's uncle.

12. Tennis is played with a ball, and hockey is played with a puck.

13. Canada is south of the United States.

14. Everybody's thumbprint is different.

15. Hilarious is another word for terrible.

16. People from England speak English.

17. If you didn't brush your teeth for three days, your teeth would turn black.

18. Valentine's Day comes in the spring.

Comment:

The note-card presentation is easy to prepare, and provides a change-of-pace from tagboard. There is a little bit about a lot for children to think about in this assignment.

Materials: Tagboard.

THE CAT'S MEOW

INSTRUCTIONS

THE CAT'S MEOW

Many of the words below have something to do with *cat*. Be careful because there are tricks. For example, nap would have something to do with a cat. . . have you ever heard of a catnap? List the words that make a connection with cat in *cursive* on your own paper.

read	school	bobby pin	bobcat
milk	door	shadow	tail
sky	fish	feline	turnip
scat	balloon	dog	please
elbow	nap	go	litter
funny	mouse	snake	catsup
nine lives	house	animal	hump
whiskers	store	hurt	tiger

Comment:

A reminder that you are looking for writing errors more than you are making judgment calls on word associations for *cat*.

MAKING VIBRATIONS

WEEK 18 SCIENCE

Materials: 6 bottles (see below), rubber bands (assorted sizes), cigar box, paper plate, lab sheet.

Experiment No. 14—Studying Vibrations Name_____

Sound comes from vibrations. Put your hand on your throat about where your Adam's apple is. Hum. Do you feel anything? You should feel some motion, or vibration. This is because your vocal cords are moving.

1. Take the cigar box and rubber bands and place them in front of you. Notice that the rubber bands are different sizes.

2. Stretch the rubber bands around the box. Strum the rubber bands. Can you hear sounds? _____

3. The rubber bands are *vibrating* when you strum them. The smallest rubber bands are stretched the most tightly and so they vibrate faster. This causes a higher sound. Try plucking the rubber bands one by one. Do you notice a difference in the sounds? _____

4. Take the rubber bands off the box and put them where you found them. Now, place the bottles in front of you.

5. Blow across the mouth of each bottle until you make a sound.

6. You will notice that each bottle has a number. Blowing across the top of each bottle again, arrange the bottles in order, from the lowest to the highest sounds.

    a. The lowest sound was made by bottle _____.

    b. Next-to-the-lowest sound was bottle _____.

    c. Then bottle _____.

    d. Then bottle _____.

    e. Then bottle _____.

    f. The highest sound was made by bottle _____.

If there is time, play some music with your bottles or the cigar box.

Comment:

    The cigar-box lid should be taken off to provide resonance.

    Bottles for the last part of this exercise should be various heights and shapes, and each should carry a number.

    Both of these music-producing experiences are on the soft side. The popular spoon-and-glass activity was rejected for decibel reasons.

Materials: Tagboard.

IT'S IN THE CARDS

I went to a bridge party last night and didn't do very well. My cards were terrible! Here is one card hand I held:

Spade ♠

Heart ♥

Diamond ♦

Club ♣

Q is a queen

J is a jack

K is a king

A is an ace

1. Starting at the left, and looking at the key for help, what is the fourth card in my hand?

2. How many hearts in my hand?

3. If an ace is the highest card and the two is the lowest, what is the next-to-the-lowest card in my hand?

4. Starting at the left, what is the eighth card in my hand?

5. Draw the symbol for a spade.

By numbers only (not by symbols), here is a bar graph of my hand.

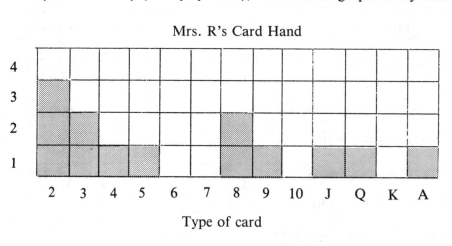

6. Which card appeared the most frequently?

7. Name the cards which appeared only once.

8. What cards appeared two times?

9. What numbers were not seen in my card hand at all?

Comment:

10. If you play cards, what games do you know how to play?

Reading charts and graphs is an important part of any work-study program. The bridge hand utilizes symbols which are made intelligible to the student through the use of a key.

The card hand can be easily graphed, also.

140

GREAT-GREAT GRANNY'S WASH

Materials: Tagboard.

Below is an old-fashioned recipe for doing the family wash. This was long before washing machines were invented, and washing had to be done by hand.

The person who wrote this probably never went to school and couldn't spell some of the words.

On your own paper, write the misspelled words the right way .

The number in parentheses lets you know how many spelling errors are in each sentence.

1. Bild a fire in the backyard to heet a kettle of rainwater. (2)

2. Set tubs so the smoke won't blow in yer eyes. (1)

3. Put one hole cake of soap in boilin water. (2)

4. Make three piles of clothes: 1 pile white, 1 pile cullord, 1 pile rags. (1)

5. Stur flour in cold water to smooth, then thin down with boilin water. (2)

6. Rub dirty spots on washboard, scub hard, then boil, rub cullord clothes but don't boil, just rench and starch. (3)

7. Take white things out of kettle with broomstick handle, then rench and starch. (1)

8. Spred towels on grass. (1)

9. Hang old rags on fence. (0)

10. Pore rench water on flower bed. (2)

11. Scub porch with hot soapy water. (1)

12. Turn tubs upside down. (0)

13. Go put on a cleen dress, smooth hair with side combs, make yourself a cup of tee—and rest and rock and count blessins. (3)

Comment:

Older children should be able to find mistakes without being told how many errors to look for in each sentence.

The recipe itself gives children an insight into what their ancestors faced. No wonder the poor author couldn't spell—she was too busy boilin and renching!

Materials: Tomato juice can with label.

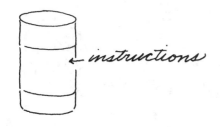

A STORY

WEEK 18 LISTENING

Materials: Story tape.

WEEK 18 CREATIVE WRITING

Materials: Construction paper (two colors).

POP	THE	QUES-TION
1.	2.	3.
4.	5.	6.
7.	8.	9.

Comment:

Be sure to enforce question marks. Also emphasize that the questions themselves should be as inventive as possible. For number three, a very ordinary question would be, "What are your two favorite colors?" A much better question would be, "What are the two most popular colors for hair?"

SEEING RED

On your own paper, make a list of every red thing which comes to your mind. Think hard, but not so hard that the blood rushes to your head. Oops, I've given you a clue.

Comment:

Put your instructions on a tomato juice can to carry out the theme.

POP THE QUESTION

The answers are given. On a separate sheet of paper, write questions which would fit the answers. Remember your question marks.

1. It's supposed to rain.

2. Math.

3. Yellow and brown.

4. Because she tattles.

5. Be a doctor.

6. He started it.

7. When I was sleeping.

8. It wasn't her fault, either.

9. It will dissolve.

Materials: White paper, crayons or markers.

tagboard

DESIGN A FLAG

INSTRUCTIONS

broom-stick or dowel

DESIGN A FLAG

The principal has asked you to do something for him (or her). You are to design a special flag for our school. The flag can have any colors you like and may include any pictures or shapes or words you like.

Remember this: The flag is to be used on top of a flagpole, so your flag must be fairly simple.

Comment:

A few words at the beginning of the week about symbols might be appropriate. You might show pictures of the flags of several nations and tell why various symbols are used. It would be interesting to have the class vote on the best design and then have volunteers actually make the flag from fabric, but. . .

Materials: Tagboard.

THE REBUS STORY

Here is a rebus story. Rebus stories use pictures in place of some words. Read this one, then write one of your own.

Once there was a boy who had a terrible temper. When he got mad, he would ☆ -t throwing 🏀-s and 🥫 -dy and even his clothes against the wall.

His mother said, "Johnny, u must 🐝 -gin to act bigger. It is 👔 -m to s- 🌰 this kind of behavior."

"O, Mom," Johnny said. "👁 would, but what makes me mad is that everybody 👃 about how mad 👁 get—and that makes me madder."

"Well, a 😁 would help," his mother said.

So he 😁 -ed and he 😁 -ed and every 👔 -m he got mad, he kept 📏 of his temper tantrums and at first, he had 100 tantrums, then 50, then 20, then 10, and finally the 😈 won! And he suddenly had friends and every day was a 🌳 -t!

NOW, IT'S YOUR TURN!

Comment:

A case could be made that rebus stories are more successfully written by children than adults. Some youngsters find picture-symbols everywhere, while the creator of the one above had to reach for hers.

Upon conclusion of this project, stories can be passed around because all children enjoy reading them.

Materials: Tagboard.

DEAR DIARY. . .

Let's test your memory. For the handwriting center today, write as much as you can about your day yesterday. . . what you wore, places you went, foods you ate, people you talked to. . . the more details in your one-day diary, the better. And, remember to write in cursive. . . naturally.

Comment:

Children of this age are too young for any sustained diary-writing, but a one-day diary is fine! They will attack this assignment with great enthusiasm. Some students (girls especially) write reams.

HOW MANY?

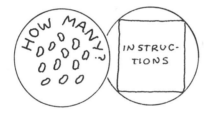

Materials: Jar of beans, extra beans, scale, ruler, pencil, paper, answer box.

Scientists often have to estimate things. To do this, they have to do more than just guess. Can you think of a way (or ways) to estimate the number of beans in this jar? Use the scale, ruler, extra beans, whatever. Put your estimate in the box. Good luck! For your information, the jar weighs three-fourths of a pound.

Comment:

Fill a jar with enough beans to make the project challenging but not so many that you exhaust yourself counting. Secure the lid with some admonishment such as, "Do Not Open This Jar."

Be sure to leave at least thirty or forty beans outside the jar. Bright children may want to weigh them to arrive at a more accurate estimate. This means that your scale should have some degree of sensitivity. You also should provide a ruler, paper, pencil and answer box.

When you introduce this center on Monday, do a good job of explaining the word *estimate*, since this is the basic concept of the assignment.

You may wish to graph the estimates prior to announcing the winner.

Materials: Tagboard.

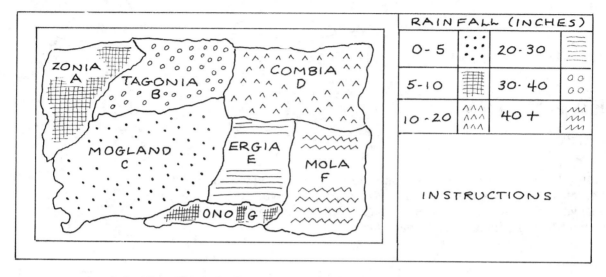

AND THE RAIN COMES DOWN

On your own paper, answer these questions.

1. Which country has the driest climate?

2. Which country has the wettest climate?

3. Which country might get seven inches of rain?

4. Which country might get 63 inches of rain?

5. Which country might get 19 inches of rain?

6. Which country might get 31 inches of rain?

7. Which countries have the same amount of rainfall?

8. Where might you expect to see cactus plants growing wild?

9. Where might you expect to see jungle plants?

10. Guess how many inches of rainfall (your state) gets every year.

11. Go to the reference section and find out how many inches of rainfall (or precipitation as it is called sometimes) (your state) receives in a year. When you find out, don't tell anybody else.

Comment:

This task is capped off by a reference back to their own territory (questions 10 and 11).

Materials: Tagboard.

FOOD SLICES

Read the special paragraph about food. You will notice that some of the words in the paragraph are underlined. When you finish reading, take out a sheet of paper and set up your paper like this:

1-syllable words	2-syllable words	3-syllable words

Then, go back and write all underlined words under the proper heading. If the word were pizza, you would place the word under the middle heading, wouldn't you?

Here is the paragraph, and don't get too hungry!

For lunch, we had chocolate mashed potatoes with turtle soup followed by jello sprinkled with horseradish. After that, we had to take some Tums for the tummy so we could get ready for dessert: grasshoppers with tomato frosting!

If you have time, think of other foods and place them under the correct heading.

Comment:

Again, the activity is extended for those who are inclined. Even though the work is syllabication, the subject is food and thus the work is rendered more interesting (though perhaps not more appetizing in this case).

Materials: Tagboard.

PATTERNS

Keep the pattern going! Figure out what is happening, then continue the pattern on your own paper. You should have as many answers as there are blanks. Problem 1, for example, should have two answers.

1. __ __

2. _ _

3. __ __

4. ABC123DE _ _

5. 100 95 90 5 10 15 85 __ __

6. 10 1 9 2 8 3 _ _ _ _

7. _

8. ____

9. __

10. ___

11. Goodbye Goodbye _____

Comment:

There will be a few children who will never be comfortable with patterns. Do not put pressure on them to "get" it. In fact, the only overriding rule for *all* work at centers is that students try.

Materials: Teacher-made tape, meter stick, centimeter ruler.

HOW LONG? HOW WIDE?

SCRIPT FOR WEEK 19

(One-minute music fade-in) Hello. Today, you are going to make yourself into an inchworm. Well, not really, but you *are* going to be doing some measuring. You are going to find out how long or how wide a few things are by using the ruler or meter stick. All answers should be rounded off to the nearest centimeter. And please remember to include the unit of measurement as well as the number. Because, if I get a paper which says nine, how do I know you're not talking about nine elephants or nine toenails? I don't mind if you abbreviate the word centimeter by writing cm. Are you ready? Listen to the instruction, stop the tape, measure, write the answer, then start the tape again. There will be seven instructions and a super-duper, extra-special bonus problem at the end. Here we go. (Pause) Number one. Measure the width of your wrist. Put your answer beside number one on your paper. (Pause) Number two. Measure the length of your nose from the top—that means between your eyes—to the tip. (Pause) Number three. Measure the height of this table at the Listening Center. (Pause) Number four. Measure the width of your math book. (Pause) Number five. Measure the length from your elbow to your fingertips. (Pause) Number six. Measure the width of the paper you are using now. (Pause) Number seven. Measure the length of the paper you are using now. (Pause) Are you ready for this? Do you have the nerve to try figuring out this difficult challenge? For extra credit, measure the thickness of the paper you are using now. Oh, oh, you say you can't? Well, there *is* a way to come close. Good listening, good measuring, good day. (One-minute music fade-out)

Comment:

A handful of youngsters may speculate that the thickness of one piece of paper may be arrived at mathematically by measuring many sheets together and then dividing.

The challenge is included to keep top students on their toes.

WEEK 19 CREATIVE WRITING

Materials: String hook-up, sales receipt or price tag for instructions.

PURCHASING POWER

Make a list of everything you have ever bought at K-Mart. If you remember what it cost, put the price, too.

Comment:

Write your instructions on a K-Mart sales receipt. Of course, you may want to substitute a drugstore or dimestore in place of K-Mart—whatever is the most popular place in your area for incidental and impulse buying.

If a student says, "Well, I didn't buy it; my mother did," assure the student that those purchases would apply, also.

WEEK 19 ART

Materials: Tagboard, paper punch, scissors, nail, yarn, string, rag strips.

THREAD UP A DESIGN

This week, we're going to make a design just for the fun of it. Here's what to do.

Use the paper punch (or scissors or the nail) to make a lot of holes in the piece of stiff paper. Then "weave" string and yarn in and out of the holes in any way you think is interesting. You can make more holes any time you like. Have fun. Make a design that is really pleasing.

You could try "threading" the word "thread" —

Comment:

This is another project which simply asks children to "play" with visual and tactile concepts. The end result may not be beautiful, and it will not be "art" in any adult sense of the word, but no matter.

Materials: Contributor's page from children's magazine, tagboard.

BY CHILDREN FOR CHILDREN

1. Who drew the fish?

2. How old was the girl who drew the boat?

3. Where does John Nelson go to school?

4. Who drew the car?

5. Which picture uses the most colors?

6. What is your favorite picture?

7. Who is the oldest artist?

Comment:

Several children's magazines devote a page to pictures sent in by young readers. A page from Children's Playmate was used for this exercise. Students gain experience in reading closely and looking for detail.

Materials: Tagboard.

HOW LONG DOES A WHALE LIVE?

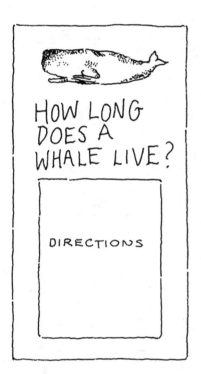

HOW LONG
DOES A
WHALE LIVE?

DIRECTIONS

*Find a good
whale
picture for
this.*

Here are some sentences about how long people and animals might expect to live. Of course, sometimes people and animals live a longer or shorter period of time, but the figures below give you an idea.

1. Humans can live 75 years.

2. Chipmunks can live 8 years.

3. Elephants can live 60 years.

4. Some turtles can live 150 years.

5. Robins can live 8 years.

6. Whales can live 30 years.

7. Parrots can live 70 years.

8. Fleas can live 1 year.

9. Some seals can live 35 years.

10. Mice can live 3 years.

In cursive, answer these questions, based on the information above.

1. Of the ten, which lives the longest?

2. How long do robins live?

3. What is the life expectancy of parrots?

4. Which fact was most surprising to you?

5. Who is your oldest relative and what is his or her age? If you don't know the age, guess.

6. In the time remaining, total up the years mentioned in all the questions. What number do you get?

Comment:

Children will want to answer these questions because the subject matter intrigues them.

STATIC ELECTRICITY

WEEK 20 SCIENCE

Materials: Balloon, flannel, bowl of paper bits, fluorescent light, two books, piece of glass, paper plate, lab sheet.

Experiment No. 15—Static Electricity   Name _____

Did you know that you can make electricity by rubbing two things together? It is called *static electricity*. It is everywhere.

PART 1

1. Rub the balloon against your hair or the flannel. Then, quickly dip the balloon into the dish of little paper pieces. How many bits of paper did you pick up on your . . .

   a. first try? _____   b. second try?_____   c. third try? _____

2. Put the pieces of paper back into the dish when you finish.

3. Now, rub the balloon against your hair or the flannel again. Then place it against the wall. Does it stay? _____
   How many seconds will it stay on the wall? _____

PART 2

4. Take the fluorescent light tube and the flannel cloth to the coat closet and rub the flannel back and forth on the light—IN THE DARK. What happens? _____

PART 3

5. Now, place a few pieces of paper from the bowl underneath the glass which is resting on two books. Rub the glass with the flannel cloth. What happens to the paper?
   _____

6. Why did the paper bits finally fall back to the table? _____

   IF THERE IS TIME, TRY RUBBING THE BALLOON AND STICKING IT ON OTHER SURFACES. LIST THE PLACES IT WILL STICK. _____

   _____

glass (edges taped)

books *paper bits*

Comment:

Take a few moments on Monday and discuss static electricity. Mention commonplace examples, such as "sliding your feet on the carpet and giving someone a shock" or "clothes sticking to you in the wintertime when the air is dry."
Children should be cautioned to carry the fluorescent tube carefully.

WEEK 20   WORK-STUDY

Materials: Dictionary. Use Week 1 presentation.

WORD FACES

Can you wear a stetson?

Would you play in a festival?

What would you do with a culotte?

Where would you find a Dutch oven?

Would you eat a sea cucumber?

Comment:

All five word faces should be in use by now, and students should find the assignment relatively easy.

WEEK 20   LANGUAGE ARTS

Materials: Use Week 14 presentation.

WORD CHISELING

Here are some more words hiding inside big words. Please "chip" them out! Do not change around the order of the letters, but you can drop letters in order to find the words. Good luck!

1. company

2. laughter

3. understanding

4. anthem

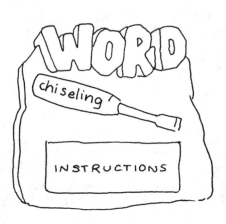

Comment:

Since youngsters have been exposed to this type of exercise once before, they should have no trouble with it this week.

ALIKE AND DIFFERENT

Materials: Tagboard.

1. How are they alike?

2. How are they different?

Comment:

The two objects are not that far removed from each other in kind. Therefore, the second question will draw the more interesting ideas.

A STORY

WEEK 20 LISTENING

Materials: Story tape.

WEEK 20 CREATIVE WRITING

Materials: 5 x 7-inch note card for instructions.

BABY BIRD TALE

It is spring. You have just found an injured baby bird. You can see it is breathing. It may be hurt just a little bit. Your mother and father are gone. Your cat is somewhere in the yard.

1. What would you do?

2. For extra credit, find out what a bird's *craw* is. What purpose does it serve?

3. For extra credit again, name as many parts of a bird as you can.

Comment:

This is another example of an incident which could very well happen to a child in real life. Thus, it has validity, and answers should be taken seriously.

155

WEEK 20 ART

Materials: Cardboard box, paper, crayons, pencil, markers.

DRAWING AN IDEA

Today, you are going to have to use your imagination. Here is what you do:

1. Reach into the box and take out *one* of the folded pieces of paper. You must take only one, and you must keep the first piece you take. No trades.

2. Unfold the paper and read the word printed on it.

3. Draw a picture which tells something about your word. The picture can have things we recognize (people, animals), or it can be a design.

Comment:

Write one of the following words on each piece of paper and fold so that the words are not visible. Cut a "hand-hole" in the cardboard box. Place folded papers in the box.

Be prepared to accept non-objective designs, symbols or realism with equal enthusiasm. Since students are being asked to provide some kind of visual equivalent for an abstract word, you should receive all kinds of solutions and learn some things about your students in the process.

Here are the words: anxious, silly, smart, mad, sad, scared, shy, gone, above, below, heavy, light, strong, weak, thinking, fussy, busy, lazy, early, late, move, easy, front, silent, noisy, gentle, difficult, far, near.

Materials: 5 x 7-inch note cards (17 needed).

FACT OR OPINION?

Some of the sentences you are about to read are facts. Some are opinions. Remember, opinions are what people think or feel. Facts are ideas that can be proven. Number from 1 to 15, then write fact or opinion after each number.

1. I think it will rain tomorrow.

2. The forecast is for rain tomorrow.

3 (Your name) needs to wash her hair.

4. Mr. (principal) is taller than (another teacher).

5. Mr. (principal) is good-looking.

6. Elephants use their trunks when taking a bath.

7. Bats are blind at birth.

8. (Your school) could use more playground equipment.

9. The best school lunch is tacos.

10. Yesterday, the mayor met with some people to discuss pollution.

11. (School secretary) is very helpful to students.

12. Homework should start in the tenth grade.

13. My older brother brought home a math assignment last night.

14. Teeth should be brushed three times a day.

15. An apple a day keeps the doctor away.

If there is time, write one opinion about school lunches and one fact about school lunches.

Comment:

Use 5 x 7-inch note cards for this assignment—one sentence to each card and directions on a separate card.

Using the principal and other teachers in sentences always makes for a good laugh.

Materials: Adult book, tagboard.

BOOKWORK

Using the book in front of you, follow these instructions. Do all of your writing in cursive!

1. Turn to page 81. Write the second and third words on the page.

2. Write the title of the book.

3. Find a word which begins with w on page 101 and write it.

4. Find a word which ends in t on page 87 and write it.

5. Write the longest word in the third paragraph on page 4.

6. Write the first word of the last paragraph on page 22.

7. Write the second sentence on page 77.

Comment:

Keep an adult book at this center this week. Children will enjoy the "prestige" of working with it. Your instructions will vary, but the tone can be the same.

OIL AND WATER

Materials: 2 glass jars, warm water, tablespoon, teaspoon, salad oil, dishwashing soap, lab sheet, paper plate.

Experiment No. 16—Oil and Water   Name _____

PART 1

1. Fill the jar halfway to the top with warm water. Add one tablespoon of salad oil and screw the lid on the jar tightly. Do not shake yet. Where is the salad oil now? _____

_____

2. Shake the jar hard. What happens to the oil? Answer this question as fully as you can.

_____

3. Set this jar aside. You will be using it later.

PART 2

4. Fill the other jar halfway to the top with warm water. Add one tablespoon of salad oil. Also, add one teaspoon of dishwashing soap. Screw the lid on tightly. Do not shake yet. Where is the oil? _____ Where is the soap?_____

_____

5. Shake the jar hard. What happens to the oil? _____

_____

PART 3

6. Compare the two jars. You should know by now which of the following sentences is true. Put a check mark by the true sentence.

    ____Water and fat blend together very easily.

    ____ Soap helps fat blend with water.

7. Why does your mother use soap in her dishwater? _____

_____

8. Wash out both jars thoroughly so that the jars will be ready for the next person.

Comment:

    By the time students get to question seven, they should know the answer.

WEEK 21 WORK-STUDY

Materials: Encyclopedia, tagboard.

FIVE FACTS

Take an encyclopedia from the reference section. Look through it. On your own paper, list five interesting things you learned.

Comment:

Take time to share the most interesting facts orally. This is a good thing to do right before lunch or at the end of the day.

WEEK 21 LANGUAGE ARTS

Materials: Tagboard.

WHO GOOFED?

Read the four sentences. They sound fine when you read them aloud, but some of the words aren't spelled right because they are homonyms. (Homonyms sound the same but can be spelled differently.)

Will *eye* be able to fool you? Write the sentence on your own paper with the correct spelling.

1. Eye dew like the blew flour the best.

2. Her hare has a read rows in it.

3. He nose what is reel oar knot.

4. The bare is won animal eye like.

If time remains, think of your own sentence, using the wrong homonyms.

Comment:

Children scramble to read these sentences because they're fun.

160

DUPS AND GLOOBHEADS

Materials: Tagboard, white drawing paper.

These are dups.

These are not dups.

1.   2.   3.   4.   5.   6.

Which of these are dups? Write the dups by number on your own paper, please.

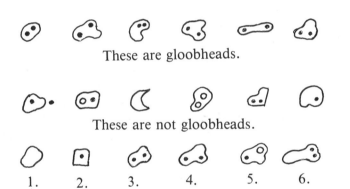

These are gloobheads.

These are not gloobheads.

1.   2.   3.   4.   5.   6.

Which of these are gloobheads? Write the gloobheads by number on your own paper, please.

If there is time, make a landscape featuring dups and gloobheads of your own.

Comment:

Dups have straight lines, blank inner spaces, and tails with two notches.

Gloobheads have two black internal circles and curved lines.

Therefore, figures 1, 4, 6 are dups; figures 3, 4, 6 are gloobheads.

The gloobhead-and-dup landscapes ideally should have figure inventions created by the students, holding true to the various characteristics above. Slower students, however, will feel more comfortable merely copying the ones already presented. That's okay. Children, after all, can only do what they can do.

Materials: Teacher-made tape.

JERRY

SCRIPT FOR WEEK 21

(One-minute music fade-in) Hello. This week, you are going to be writing some of your opinions. First, though, number your paper from one to five and leave a big space after each number. (Pause) Now, let's talk for a moment about Jerry. Jerry is a boy who knows *everything*. Whenever the teacher asks a question, Jerry is the first one with his hand up. He has an opinion about every subject. Not only that, he always is *sure* that he's right. But *nobody* can be right all the time, not even Jerry. The teacher tries to call on other people first, but Jerry keeps his hand up, anyway. And, if the teacher does not get around to calling on him, he goes into a hand-waving and snorting routine that is really something to see. Beside number one on your paper, write what you think about Jerry and other people who try to draw attention to themselves at school this way. (Pause) There's another side to Jerry that other kids don't know. At home, he really has a tough life. His dad can't hold a job, and so his mother has to work. She is gone most of the time, therefore. This leaves Jerry and his brother, Sam, and their dad together quite often. Sometimes, Jerry's dad starts feeling sorry for himself and, when this happens, he takes out his bad feelings on his sons. It's hard on the two boys. Underneath it all, Jerry has a pretty poor opinion of himself because he really doesn't think his dad likes him. Also, they live out on the edge of town, so there isn't much to do. There is one thing to do, however—read books. And Jerry likes to read. Jerry reads because books take him to different places—places that help him escape from his real life. The most favorite place he's ever been—in books—is on the Mississippi with Huckleberry Finn. He wouldn't want to let other kids know it, but books and school are the brightest spots in his day. In school, he can try hard, and he almost always knows the answer. Still, though, he feels that his teacher hasn't been as nice to him lately. He's a little worried about it. He will just have to try even harder, get his hand up quicker and higher, so that he can please the teacher. One day, he goes to school and he's really wound up. He interrupts others in his haste to talk. He groans and moans when he raises his hand for her to recognize him. As for the teacher, she has just about had it. In front of everyone, she tells him to stay in for recess because she wants to talk to him. Stop the tape and, beside number two, *you* be the teacher and write what you think she should say to him. (Pause) The teacher didn't tell him anything, at first. She asked questions. She asked him what was bothering him, and she did find out a little bit about his problems at home. And then, she began to understand why he tried so hard, *too* hard, at school, and why he interrupted and seemed to know everything all the time. With this understanding, she explained to him what he was doing wrong. She told him what he was doing *right*, also. Then, they worked out a little plan. If Jerry began to talk too much or wave his hand in the air, she crossed two of her fingers as a special sign for him to remember. The hand signals worked. Pretty soon, he seemed more relaxed, and he also started making some new friends. What he never did find out was that one day the teacher sent Jerry on an errand to the office so she could talk to the class. She told the class about some of Jerry's problems. She asked the class to help him. Do you think the teacher should have done that? Why or why not? Stop the tape and put your answer beside number three. (Pause) Can you remember how many brothers Jerry had? Can you remember the name or names? Put your answer beside number four. (Pause) Jerry worked out his problems because he had the help of other students and the teacher. He even became quite popular. Let's face it, some kids seem to have more friends than others. Some kids seem easier to like than other kids. Of course, every single person is valuable. But what qualities make some children so well-liked? Turn off the tape and write a few words about what makes children popular. Good listening and good day. (One-minute music fade-out)

Comment:

Even though children have not reached Piaget's formal reasoning stage, they are able to *sense* ambivalence in complex situations. You will notice that this assignment goes from the specific (Jerry's overbearing nature) to the general (popularity).

Materials: Ball or apple, string hook-up.

EVERYTHING ROUND

Make a list of everything in this room which is round.

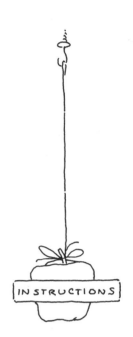

Comment:

Write your instructions directly on a ball or tape a label on an apple.

It is surprising how many round shapes can be found in one room. A clever student may come up with "faces" as an answer and be twenty or more answers ahead of everyone else. . . Jack's face, Bonnie's face, Brad's face, etc.

BURP!

Materials: White paper, colored markers or crayons.

Pretend you are very, very hungry. What is your favorite meal? What would it look like if it were all spread out and ready to eat?

Use the markers and make a picture that looks good enough to eat. Be sure to fill up the paper.

Comment:

This should provide some interesting results. There could be nutrition or creative-writing possibilities in connection with this project.

Materials: Colored worksheet,
candy.

HAPPY EASTER

1. Your name written in your fanciest cursive. _____

2. In ten minutes, make as many small words as you can out of the phrase
   Happy Easter. _____

   _____

   _____

3. Stand up, turn around twice and sit down.

4. Wink at the teacher.

5. Write your plans for Easter vacation. _____

   _____

   _____

6. Tiptoe up to the blackboard, make a face at it, then tiptoe back.

7. Whistle once.

8. Write your name backwards. _____

9. Walk up to (your name) and shake her hand.

10. Go over to the storage cabinet, lift the lid of the small box, and take
    one of whatever is in it.

11. Do not tell anybody about this center this week. Will you keep the
    surprise secret? Promise?

12. Do have a happy vacation.

Comment:

Put this on a colored worksheet, provide a
small treat, and get in the vacation spirit. Be
sure to include all students in the class for this
activity.

Materials: Tagboard.

WHAT's for SUPPER?
L

INSTRUCTIONS

Decorate with
food pictures

WHAT'S FOR LUPPER?

Copy this paragraph in cursive:

A meal which is halfway between breakfast and lunch is called brunch. Does that mean that a meal halfway between lunch and dinner is a dunch? Or, if you call dinner by the name of supper, a meal between lunch and supper would be called lupper.

If there is time, answer these questions. Do your answers in cursive.

1. What would be a good name for an animal which is half donkey, half rabbit?

2. What would be a good name for an animal which is part worm and part cat?

3. Can you draw the animals in Number 1 and 2?

Comment:

Children may want to think of some additional hybrid words.

WEEK 22 SCIENCE

Materials: Hand mirror, glass, picture of a person, white paper for drawing through glass, carbon paper, typing paper, ballpoint pen, lab sheet, paper plate, sign.

REFLECTIONS

Experiment No. 17—Reflections   Name_____

PART 1

1. Pick up the hand mirror and hold it so you can see your face. Wink with your left eye. Smile twice. What you are seeing is the reflection of yourself. The "picture" of you is hitting the mirror and being reflected back to your eyes.

2. Now, hold up the sign. What happens to the writing? _____

_____

3. Place a piece of the small white paper on one side of the clear glass. The drawing of the man is on the other side. Position the glass so that the drawing is nearest to you. Reaching over the glass with the pencil in hand, draw the reflection you see on the white paper. How is your drawing different from the other drawing? _____

PART 2

4. Lay the piece of carbon paper dark-side-up on the table. Put one piece of typing paper over it. Write some words on the paper with the ballpoint pen.

5. Turn over your paper and you will see reversed writing.

6. Read the reversed writing in the hand mirror. Can you read it? What has happened? ____

7. If there is time, you may want to do more reverse writing.

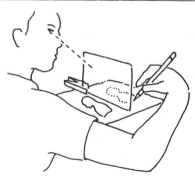

Comment:

The reflected drawing is achieved by taking a small piece of glass or plastic and standing it upright with a clothespin, as shown in the illustration. It is best to tape the picture to one side of the glass in advance, so that children will know where the white paper goes. Tape the edges of the glass to avoid cuts.

You also need to make a sign for part 1.

DICTIONARY GOOSE HUNT

WEEK 22 WORK-STUDY

Materials: Dictionary. Use Week 13 presentation.

Begin with the word spank. Look up the word in the dictionary. Write the first five words of meaning 1.

Next, look up a word which begins with the *second* letter in spank. Write that word plus the first five words of meaning 1.

What is the second letter in your new word? Find another word which begins with it. Also, write the first five words of the definition.

Do this again (using the second letter) and again.

Now, use all five words in a long sentence.

Comment:

Students have had a similar exercise.

WANDERING WORDS

WEEK 22 LANGUAGE ARTS

Materials: Colored worksheet.

Wandering Words   Name_____

See how many four-letter words you can make by changing *one letter at a time* in the words below. Look at the example before you begin.

r	e	a	l
s	e	a	l
s	e	a	m
b	e	a	m
b	e	a	r
d	e	a	r
p	e	a	r
p	e	a	s

b	a	l	l

s	a	n	d

f	a	c	e

b	o	o	k

Comment:

Procedural matters are taken care of when the activity is put on a worksheet. Use colored paper, please.

Materials: Colored worksheet.

CATEGORIES

Directions: Fill in as many of the spaces as you can by looking at the top of the column for the topic and to the left of each row for the beginning letter of the word you will be making. The example should help you. Some of the boxes might be difficult. Try your best.

	Toys	Food	Occupations	Countries
S	soldier	sandwich		
W				
A				
M				
P				

Comment:

The worksheet format is best. Use colored stock. Reference materials may be used if children desire.

A STORY

WEEK 22 LISTENING

Materials: Story tape.

Materials: Animal pictures, instruction card, tagboard.

FOR OR AGAINST?

How do you feel about zoos? Scientists called zoologists use zoos to study wild animals. We go to zoos for the fun of seeing animals we might never see otherwise and to learn about animals, too.

Animals in zoos have been taken away from their natural environment. Sometimes, their behavior changes. A lion, for example, doesn't have to go out and kill for food because food is given to him by the zookeeper. So he might forget about knowing how to hunt.

1. Write a brief paragraph about whether you are for or against zoos.

2. Have you ever been to a zoo? If you have, where was it and what did you see?

3. If you were starting a zoo, and could have just five kinds of animals, what would they be?

Comment:

This project translates very nicely to the bulletin board. Make some vertical bars out of tagboard, put a few pictures of animals behind the bars, superimpose answers to question one. . . and you have an effective display coming from the students themselves. The assignment encourages children to think critically.

WEEK 22 ART

Materials: Crayons, markers, white paper.

Use a couple of hexagons for this. No motorcycle or dress photos.

BE A DESIGNER

Take your choice. Design the neatest car or motorcycle you can *or* an outfit you might wear on a very special occasion.

Comment:

This project comes complete with its own motivation, so just stand back and enjoy the results.

WEEK 22   READING

Materials: Use Week 3 presentation.

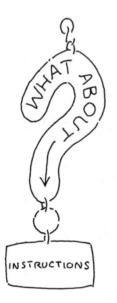

WHAT ABOUT. . . A FISH'S EYE?

1. Take the new Childcraft Book Number 5 to your desk and turn to page 70. Read it.

2. Then answer these questions.

   A. What is strange about a fish's eye?

   B. What are gills?

   C. Have you ever gone fishing? What have you caught? What bait did you use? What was your largest fish?

   D. If there is time—and if you know—give directions for baiting a hook.

Comment:

If you hand an encyclopedia to a child and say "read it," he probably would use it carelessly. Not so when you direct him to an assigned page.

Materials: Tagboard.

I SENTENCE YOU. . .

In cursive, make up and write:

1. One question.

2. One sentence which describes some object in the room.

3. One sentence which describes a person in the room.

4. One sentence which is about something happy.

5. One goofy sentence.

6. One sentence which begins this way: I wish that. . . .

Comment:

   You may wish to turn the second and third sentences into guessing games for the whole class.

Materials: Adding machine tape,
centimeter ruler, string, pencil,
meter stick, lab sheet, paper plate.

MAKE A MEASURING TAPE

Experiment No. 18 — Measuring Tape   Name _____

In front of you is a string, a centimeter ruler, scissors, adding machine tape and a pencil. You are going to make your own measuring device today—a one-meter tape. Follow directions carefully and work slowly.

1. Using the centimeter ruler, cut your string so that it is ten centimeters long.

2. Set the ruler aside. Now, take the adding machine tape and place the string upon it.

3. Mark the distance of one string (ten centimeters) on the tape. Repeat until you get a ten-string measure. This should mean you have a tape which is one-meter long. Cut the adding machine tape when you reach this point.

4. Go to the supply closet and bring back the meter stick. Compare your tape with the meter stick. How did you do? _____

   If you were short or long, write down the number of centimeters you were off by.
   _____

5. Why was it hard to be accurate? _____

   _____

6. Put the meter stick back in the closet, put your name on the tape and hand it in, please.

Comment:

   After the children make their tapes, they will understand why we have standard units of measurement.

   It is helpful to cut lengths of adding machine paper, rather than have students work from the whole roll.

Materials: Map section, tagboard.

GO READ A MAP

Look at the map. Then answer these questions.

1. North Carolina borders on what large body of water?

2. Name three towns or cities which begin with a W.

3. Name one river found on this map.

4. Name one of the largest cities. How did you know it was a large city? (Two answers are required for this problem, please)

5. Interstate Highway 95 runs mainly north and _____.

6. Name one national forest.

7. If you were taking an afternoon trip out of Lumberton, where might you go?

Comment:

   Do not use too large a map section. Try to choose an area which has varied features, such as rivers, an ocean, big and small towns, interstate highways. Be sure to include a directional sign, also.
   Your questions will be different, but *do* use the idea expressed in question seven.

Materials: Tagboard.

SPRINGTIME

Think spring. Read the clues and write your answers on your own paper.

S _ _ _ _ _   Important marble.

Girls jump _ _ P _

_ _ R _ _ First month of spring.

_ I _ _ _ _ Popular transportation for children in the spring.

N _ _ _ _ Bird homes.

G _ _ _ What plants do in the spring (verb).

T _ _ _ _ _ Early spring flowers.

_ _ I _ _ What children do to trees sometimes.

The grass needs M _ _ _ _ _

_ _ _ E _ _ _ _ Three strikes and you're out—a game.

Comment:

The answers are: steelie, rope, March, bicycle, nests, grow, tulips, climb, mowing, baseball.

ELECTRIFYING   ASSIGNMENT

Materials: Extension cord with instructions attached.

instructions

Think of your house. Think of every room in your house. Then, going room-by-room, think of every single thing which runs on electricity. Do a good job. Better start with the kitchen!

Comment:

Attach your instructions to an extension cord to carry out the theme of this week's assignment.

WORD BEAN DIP

Materials: Teacher-made tape, alphabet word beans.

SCRIPT FOR WEEK 23

(One-minute music fade-in) Hello, boys and girls. Today, we will be working with the alphabet word beans. Please follow directions carefully. The first direction is easy. Number your paper from one to five, leaving a big space between each number. (Pause) Stop the tape between questions. Ready? Here we go. Begin by measuring out two scoops of beans. Do this now. (Pause) On your paper beside number one, list any nouns or pronouns you find in these two scoops. (Pause) Now, measure out three scoops of beans. (Pause) Write the longest sentence you can, beside number two. (Pause) Next, measure out five scoops of beans. (Pause) Beside number three, list all the two-syllable words you find. (Pause) Measure out three scoops of beans. (Pause) Put all words beginning with *a* together, all words beginning with *b* together, and so forth. Then, write on your paper, beside number four, the words in your biggest group. (Pause) Measure out four scoops of beans. (Pause) This time, group these words *not* by the beginning letter but in *another* way. You decide. Then, on your paper beside number five, write how you chose to group your beans. That's it for today. Happy listening, happy beaning, happy day. (Two-minute music fade-out)

Comment:

You will notice that the last two directions involve classifying.

SOUR THOUGHTS

Materials: Tagboard.

Write down every sour thing in the world. Then, write one sour sentence and make it look like a poem, putting one word only on each line. Let the example help you.

Example: Lemons burst in my mouth like little shooting stars.

> Lemons
> burst
> in
> my
> mouth
> like
> little
> shooting
> stars.

Comment:

The "sour" lists set the stage for very simple poetry-writing. As previously stated, most children of this age are not ready to write poetry in any adult sense of the word.

There may be a few children who will write more than one "sour" poem or who will want to deviate from this form and experiment. Hallelujah.

SPRING THING

Materials: Construction paper, paste, scissors, markers.

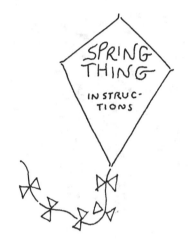

This week, we're all going to work together to dress up our bulletin board. Think of all the things that happen in the spring—flowers, insects, new leaves, birds, kites, outdoor games. Then, make some nice spring things and add them to the bulletin board.

Comment:

You provide the format. Use colored paper to create a landscape with plenty of green grass and blue sky. Perhaps you will want to cut out the words "Spring Things" and use them as part of the display. Then, simply let the children fill up the landscape with their spring creations.

WEEK 23   READING

BATTER UP!

Materials: 5 baseball cards, tagboard.

On a separate piece of paper, answer the following questions.

1. If Rudy Meoli plays for the Cubs and Dave Collins plays for the Mariners, who does Bump Wills play for?

2. Rudy Meoli is a shortstop. Bump Wills plays at _____ base.

3. What is the height of Jeff Burroughs?

4. Bump Wills is the son of _____.

5. Pete Falcone plays for what club?

6. Dave Collins weighs _____ pounds.

7. Jeff Burroughs hit a _____ in the ninth inning at Atlanta.

8. If you play baseball, what position do you like to play? Why? If you do not play baseball, write a paragraph about your favorite sport.

Comment:

You can obtain baseball cards from certain brands of bubble gum.

One card should be pasted picture-side-up, while the other four are pasted information-side-up.

Baseball cards contain a wealth of statistical information, and thus provide good practice in locating detail.

Materials: Tagboard.

yellow and white tagboard

WHAT'S COOKING?

Explain how you would fry an egg. Be sure to include every detail, every step. You should use words like *first, next, then,* and *finally.* Or you could number the steps.

Do your writing in cursive.

Comment:

Later, you might read to the class the "ideal" set of directions: Get out a skillet about eight inches in diameter and put it on the burner. Put in one tablespoon of butter and turn the heat to medium-high. When the butter melts and gets bubbly, break an egg carefully into the skillet. Turn the heat down to medium-low. Cook the egg for just a minute or two. If you like a sunnyside-up egg, cook until the white is done the way you like it. If you like your egg over-easy, gently turn it over with a spatula and cook for just another minute or two.

Materials: 3 pocket-sized mirrors, adhesive tape, paper with guide-lines, checker, bowl of colored paper pieces, piece of orange construction paper, lab sheet and clothespin.

MIRRORS

Experiment No. 19—Mirrors   Name_____

PART 1

In front of you are two mirrors which have been taped together so they can open and close like a book.

1. Set the mirrors on the paper so that the bottom edges touch the red lines. Now, place the checker between the mirrors. How many checkers do you see? _____

2. Change the angle of the mirrors by putting the bottom edges on the green line. How many checkers do you see now? _____

3. Put the mirrors on the brown lines. How many checkers now? _____

4. Can you explain why the number of images changes?

PART 2

5. Reach into the bowl and help yourself to some colored bits of paper. Put these on the large piece of orange paper. Now, set your two mirrors behind the colored bits. Change the angle and you'll make different designs. What kind of toy is somewhat like this?

PART 3

6. If there is time, you might like to do some mirror writing. Use the single mirror for this. Look in the mirror and try to write so that you can read your writing *in the mirror*. This means you will have to write backwards.

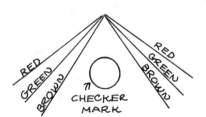

Comment:

Two pocket-sized mirrors can be hinged easily with book or adhesive tape for Part 1 of this project. You also need to draw red, green and brown lines on a piece of paper so that children can set the mirrors at various angles, thus producing a differing number of images.

The toy in Part 2 is a kaleidoscope.

Attach a spring clothespin to the base of one pocket-sized mirror for Part 3, and it will stand easily.

Materials: Black tagboard, white paper.

BLACK!

There are many expressions which have to do with black. Look up the word black in the dictionary. Do you see all the words which begin with black? Then, answer the questions. All underlined words are in the dictionary.

1. If a policeman is carrying a blackjack, what kind of a weapon is it? (meaning 3)

2. If you are asked to play blackjack, what would you need? (meaning 5)

3. If you are black and blue, what has happened to your skin?

4. Does a black hole have something to do with mountains, land or the sky?

5. A black-eyed Susan is a girl, a dog, or a flower?

6. What would happen to you if you suffered a blackout? (meaning 1)

7. What would happen to your house if there were a blackout? (meaning 3)

8. What does a blacksmith do?

9. A synonym for black magic is _____.

10. If someone blackmailed you, would you be happy or sad? (meaning 2)

11. What workers most likely would get blacklung?

12. Would you want to be on my blacklist? Why or why not?

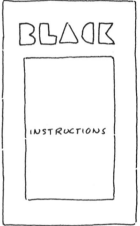

Use white paper on black tagboard.

Comment:

Your questions may differ slightly, depending on your dictionary.

Materials: Class list, tagboard.

NAME DROPPING

Looking at the list, answer these questions. Be sure to include *every* first name which would answer the question. Examples are in parentheses.

1. Whose names start with a consonant blend? (Steve)

2. Whose names start with a digraph? (Charles)

3. Whose names have long vowel sounds? (Brice)

4. Whose names have double consonants? (Bill)

5. Whose names have a short e? (Betty)

6. Whose names have one syllable? (Al)

Comment:

Provide students with a class list this week, and let them do the rest. Being little egomaniacs, they respond to this personalized exercise where they might groan over a more perfunctory one.

Materials: Tagboard.

BRAINSPRINKLE

1. A bed has a foot. What else has a foot?

2. A pin has a head. What else has a head?

3. A needle has an eye. What else has an eye?

4. What is wrong with this sentence?

> When we go to the
> the party, every-
> body stares at me.

5. If you wanted to make stilts, what would you need?

6. Draw a picture of a person on stilts.

Comment:

There are Brainsprinkles and there are Brainsprinkles. Number four of this Brainsprinkle will drive youngsters to distraction. The error, of course, is that there are two *the's* in the sentence.

A STORY

Materials: Story tape.

Materials: Instruction card.

PROBLEMS, PROBLEMS

Pretend you are a third-grade boy and you have a problem. Kids tease you and sometimes you cry. You don't mean to cry, and when you do, you get mad at yourself later. But, every time kids start calling you names, you can't stop the tears from coming.

Your dad says to be tough—to use your fists. However, there is a school rule: no fighting. You do have one very good friend, but he's moving. The problem probably is going to get worse.

1. What is the main problem?

2. What are some of the other problems?

3. Is it wrong not to want to fight?

4. Are nicknames always bad?

Comment:

Students are not asked to come up with solutions. Instead, they are being challenged to sort out the issues—a basic process which should precede problem-solving, anyway.

The third and fourth questions deal with social pressures which affect many children from elementary age on.

Materials: Pencil, paper, crayons.

EYES CLOSED!

Who says you're too old to scribble?

This week you are going to make a picture which begins with a scribble. Here is what you do.

1. Take a clean piece of paper and lay it flat on the table.

2. Hold the paper with one hand, and pick up a pencil in the other.

3. Close your eyes.

4. Now, while you are counting to ten, scribble some big loops and other shapes on your paper. Then, open your eyes.

5. What do you see? A mess? Probably. Well, don't worry. Your job now is to look at all those messy scribbles and try to think of something they remind you of. It might be an elephant, an airplane, a duck, a doughnut. . . anything.

6. Using crayons or markers, turn the scribbles into a drawing of something we can recognize.

Comment:

This takes advantage of a very natural impulse and gives it legitimacy!

Materials: Tagboard.

READING DIRECTIONS

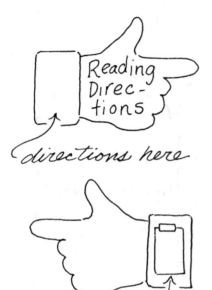

1. Read all directions carefully before you begin to write.

2. Number your page from 1 to 10. Skip a line between each number.

3. Write the number 345 next to number 6.

4. Put three circles next to number 10.

5. Draw two flowers on the line marked 4.

6. Write the word dog on line 7.

7. Put 12 question marks on line 2.

8. Write this on line 5: Sally sells seashells at the seashore.

9. Write the name of your favorite television show on line 8.

10. Put your name at the top of your paper, ignore directions 1-9, (ignore means *don't do*) and hand in your paper.

11. Look under the flap on the back of this paper.

Comment:

On the reverse side of the assignment sheet, fashion a flap. Beneath the flap, write: If you are good at following directions, the only thing on your paper should be your name.

You will get a lot of sheepish reactions, including some papers which show evidence of hasty erasures. Ignore this minor "cheating." The point has been made.

Materials: Tagboard.

BiG LITTLE GNATS

In the following story, you are asked to use antonyms in place of the underlined words *as you write the story in cursive.*

I hate <u>little</u> gnats. Some are <u>tall</u>. Some are <u>thin</u>. Some are very <u>hairy</u>. Some fly <u>fast</u> and make <u>loud</u> noises. Some <u>whisper</u> as they buzz around my ears. Some fly <u>up</u> my nose and <u>into</u> my eyes.

Gnats are <u>bad</u>. They are <u>mean</u>, <u>dumb</u> and <u>dirty</u>. I caught one once and put it under a <u>microscope</u>. Now <u>I know why gnats are</u> <u>bad</u>. Each one of them has <u>big</u> teeth and wears a <u>frown</u>.

Comment:

Handwriting is combined with language arts, and why not? If children remember what an antonym is, and if they have mastered their cursive writing, they are home free!

Materials: Paint shirt, small (¼-cup) measuring container of water, black ink, can of household oil, saucer, cardboard, string, dish, blue-yellow-red chalk, spoon, lab sheet, paper plate, waste jar.

EXPERIMENT WITH COLOR

Experiment No. 20—Color   Name_____

   Everybody has seen colors in a rainbow. Some of you probably have seen colors when sunlight hits a spray of water a certain way. Colors are everywhere, aren't they? Today, we are going to combine some colors which will then make new colors.

PART 1

1. Put on the paint shirt because the liquids you will be using could stain your clothes.

2. Fill the measuring cup with water and pour it into the saucer.

3. Color the water with black ink until it is very dark.

4. Add one drop of oil to the water in the saucer, dropping the oil at the edge nearest you.

5. What happens? _____

6. Blow on the surface and the colors will change.

7. Pour the liquid into the waste container when you are finished.

PART 2

8. Take the cardboard circle which has yellow on one side, blue on the other. Twirl it.
   What color do you see now? _____

PART 3

9. Take a tiny piece of blue chalk and a tiny piece of yellow chalk. Put them in the dish.
   Crush them with the spoon and mix them. What color do you get? _____

10. Repeat, using blue and red chalk. What color do you get? _____

Run string through middle of spinner

Comment:

   The experiment in Part I can stain clothes, so a protective covering should be provided. It is recommended that this experiment take place in strong light but not in direct sunlight. Have the saucer, water and ink already there—do not expect a child to carry a full saucer clear across the room. A few drops of ink will suffice. Have a "waste" jar handy for disposal of the ink water.

   The yellow-blue spinner for Part 2 is easy to make. Use tempera paint on two layers of cardboard which have been stapled together, or cover the cardboard with colored paper.

Materials: Dictionary. Use Week 1 presentation.

WORD FACES

Each of these faces is telling you a new word. First, look at the word in the mouth and write it on your own paper. Next to the word, answer the question on the face. You need to look up the word in the dictionary to be able to answer the question.

Where would you find an endive?

What would you do with a kimono?

Can you wear an ibex?

Would you play in a glade?

Would you eat a parsonage?

Comment:

Let's hope they don't eat a parsonage.

WEEK 25 LANGUAGE ARTS

Materials: Use Week 8 presentation.

I EAT. . . SKY AND SPACE WORDS

I Eat. . . Words about sky and space.

Comment:

The "mouth" is used for this project. Children have no trouble with the subject, thanks to Star Wars, Star Trek and other galactic experiences.

Materials: Use Week 12 presentation.

BRAINSTORMING

1. Think of five things which make sounds. Write them on your paper.

2. Circle one of the words you just wrote and then make a new list of five objects which express your circled word.

3. Do this two more times, so that you end up with 20 words in all.

If there is time, make a drawing based on five of your words.

Example: five weather words—

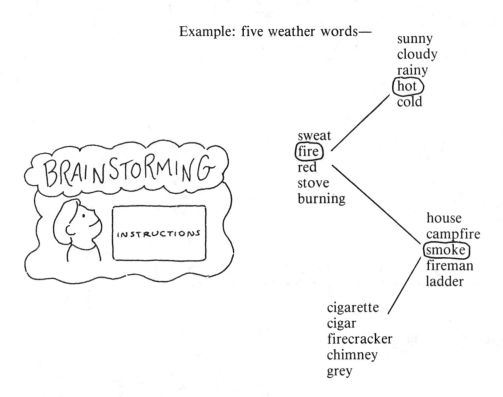

sunny
cloudy
rainy
(hot)
cold

sweat
(fire)
red
stove
burning

house
campfire
(smoke)
fireman
ladder

cigarette
cigar
firecracker
chimney
grey

Comment:

The children have done this before. The pencil drawings need not be "precious." Have them use the back of their paper.

RADIAL SYMMETRY

Materials: Teacher-made tape, paper bag, half an orange, box with Tinkertoys, drawing of bullseye.

SCRIPT FOR WEEK 25

(One-minute music fade-in) Hello, boys and girls. In the paper bag is an object which you will be working with today; but before you peek, number your paper from one to four and leave plenty of space between the numbers. (Pause) Remember, you can stop the tape at any time to do your thinking and writing. (Pause) Now, reach into the bag and take out the object. What is it? Yes, it is half an orange. The plastic wrap is on it to protect it, so please do not remove the wrapping. The purpose of using an orange today is to introduce two new words which you probably have not heard before. They are: *radial symmetry*. An orange has radial symmetry. This means there is a center and from the center are lines which come out, or radiate, from it. Another example of this would be the way a lot of children draw the sun. They make a circle, and then they draw straight lines all the way around the circle, coming out from the middle. Which makes, by the way, a perfectly good sun! Now, beside number one, I want you to make a list of other objects which have radial symmetry. Think of foods, transportation, plants, everything. I'll give you a hint to get you started. How about a bicycle wheel? Wouldn't that be a good example of radial symmetry? Stop the tape and make your list. (Pause) There is also a box at this center this week. Remove the lid and bring out the contents. Yes, you see something very familiar. Many of you have them at home, don't you? I want you to take the Tinkertoys and make an object which would express radial symmetry. In other words, make a middle and make every line come out from the middle. Do this now. Then, when you are finished, draw around your object onto the paper beside number two, so I can see what you did. (Pause) Speaking of radial symmetry, what part of the face comes closest to having radial symmetry? I'll give you a list of face parts to choose from: forehead, eyebrows, eyes with eyelashes, nose, mouth, chin, teeth, ears. Which one would be the most like radial symmetry—although it isn't quite? Put your answer by number three. (Pause) Another brainteaser. A bullseye does *not* give us an example of radial symmetry. On the lid of the box, you see that I've drawn a bullseye. Study it. Why doesn't the bullseye have radial symmetry? Put your answer beside number four. In the time remaining, play with the Tinkertoys. Good listening and good day. (One-minute music fade-out)

Comment:

This is one of the more ambitious listening activities, because the concept of radial symmetry is somewhat advanced. (It is "gettable," though.)

Note that you need to draw a bullseye on the top of the Tinkertoy box.

WEEK 25 CREATIVE WRITING

Materials: Construction paper (two colors).

POP	THE	QUES-TION
1.	2.	3.
4.	5.	6.
7.	8.	9.

Comment:

The answers are a bit more evasive this time, making the phrasing of the questions more difficult.

POP THE QUESTION

The answers are given. You write the questions. Remember your question marks.

1. An elephant.

2. Because it's boring.

3. Quarter to three in the morning.

4. Five and eleven.

5. Well, I was hungry.

6. I didn't have any money.

7. I don't want to tell her.

8. Eighty-seven.

9. Because I do!

WEEK 25   ART

Materials: Black felt marker, white paper.

DRAW A GRASSHOPPER

Take a close look at the photograph of the grasshopper. Study it carefully. Then, using the black marker pen, make a big drawing of the grasshopper. Put in as much detail as you can, and try to fill up the page.

Comment:

Your better students generally will make more detailed drawings.

If no grasshopper photographs are available, change the name of this project to Cricket, Cockroach, whatever.

The use of black ink on white paper provides a strong, graphic look which makes an interesting display.

Materials: Tagboard.

THE K SOUND

In this story, there are ten words which have the K sound. On your paper, write them. Then, figure out the riddles.

The Story

The best food in the world is crackers. Because they are so crunchy! But in order for them to be crunchy, they must be very fresh and crisp. Crackers can't be left unopened for very long. Wrap them up carefully, and they will keep for a long time. Besides, it keeps them away from cats.

Riddles

What word begins with a K and means:

1. An animal that carries her baby in her pocket.

2. An important man who wears jewels on his head.

3. Something done with the lips and making a smacking noise.

4. A metal object used to open a door or to start a car.

Comment:

If, in your teaching, you refer to the K sound as the hard C sound, be sure to modify this material. This project has been placed at the Reading Center this week; but obviously, it is multi-disciplinary, as many of the centers are.

Materials: Adult book, tagboard.

IT'S IN THE BOOK

Using the book in front of you, follow the instructions and do all your writing in cursive.

1. Turn to page 40 and write the first word on that page.

2. Write the third word from the bottom on page 87.

3. Find the author's name and write it.

4. Write the longest word in the second paragraph on page 14.

5. Write the twelfth word on page 9.

6. Write the last sentence in the book.

7. Write the last word in number 6 backwards.

8. Find and write three verbs (action words) on page 11.

Comment:

Use an adult book for this assignment. It is best to choose a page which *begins* with a paragraph for number four to make the "second paragraph" instruction very clear.

STUDYING

BALANCE

Materials: 2 yardsticks, string or cord, ruler, bowl of checkers, lab sheet, paper plate.

Experiment No. 21—The Study of Balance Name_____

PART 1

1. Pick up the yardstick.

2. Rest the stick on your two forefingers like this: ___

3. Starting with your fingers near the ends of the stick, slide your fingers toward the center.

4. Where do the fingers meet on the yardstick—before the stick falls to the floor?

_____

PART 2

5. By now, you should have made an interesting discovery—that the balance of things is to be found near the *middle*. Let's try something else. Put the ruler through the loop of string which is hanging from the other yardstick.

6. When the ruler is in no danger of falling, it is in balance. Where is the loop of string when this happens? _____

PART 3

7. Take two checkers from the bowl.

8. Put one on each end of the ruler which has been balanced. Can you do it?

9. Take four checkers from the bowl. Put them on the ruler. Can you do it?

10. There is a way to put five checkers on the ruler without the ruler falling to the floor. Can you do this? (Think of a heavy person and a light person sitting on a seesaw. What does the heavy person have to do?) _____

Comment:

Very basic materials are needed for this project. The simple balance is achieved by putting some weight on one end of a yardstick and suspending a cord which has a fairly tight loop on the end, as shown in the illustration.

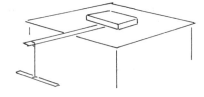

Materials: Dictionary, tagboard.

DIGGING INTO THE DICTIONARY

cookie, (kook´e), n. 1. any of various small, sweet, flat or slightly raised cakes. 2. an attractive woman. 3. a very tough person. Pl. cookies.

DIGGING INTO THE DICTIONARY

INSTRUCTIONS

Read the definition of *cookie* carefully. On your own paper, answer these questions.

1. How many different meanings are there?

2. Kook´e gives the reader two important pieces of information. What are they?

3. The first definition is usually the most common. Write a sentence using the word cookie with that meaning.

4. What does pl. stand for?

5. What does n. mean?

6. Which meaning fits this sentence? I knew right away we would have to be careful because we were dealing with a very tough cookie. (Write the number of the meaning which fits.)

7. You are a dictionary writer. You have been given the word <u>store</u> to put in the dictionary. Following the cookie example, try to write an entry for <u>store</u>—without help from a real dictionary.

8. Now, look up <u>store</u> in the dictionary and see how the dictionary entry compares with yours. How did you do?

Comment:

Standard pronunciation symbols have not been used in this assignment because my students weren't familiar enough with them to work with the symbols independently. Moreover, the learning strategy as a whole is more important than this one rather minor aspect. Asking students to write a dictionary entry of their own is the key principle here. When they can do this, you know they understand the many functions of a dictionary.

The students will be in for a surprise when they look up *store* in the dictionary and find that it is a verb as well as a noun. It keeps them humble!

Materials: Tagboard.

YOUR BLOOK IS YOPPIRNG!

As you know, the *subject* is the *who* or *what* of the sentence. Keep this in mind as you read the nonsense sentences below. Even though some of the words are not real words, you should be able to tell what the subject (or subjects) is by the way it appears in the sentence.

Copy each subject on your own paper.

1. Every slark is an unboodle.

2. The ziltz was stohing the merlzish.

3. Three lils were zipeqing pykets!

4. The ypl and rys gave the gorpy some hortz.

5. A pretty pqwrrl is like a nooper.

6. The zoup setyup goes to the puonper.

7. Q like a cyqoooper—now and then.

Comment:

If they can find the subject under these rather unconventional circumstances, they are sure to know a real one when they see it.

The subject of number seven, of course, is Q—which functions as an "I" would.

Materials: Use Week 4 presentation.

IDEAS THAT ARE ALIKE

Below are pairs of words which are alike in some way. You must figure out what makes them alike and add one more word to each set.

1. Growl, purr, _____

2. Apple, banana, _____

3. Velvet, cotton, _____

4. Maple, cottonwood, _____

5. Elbow, wrist, _____

6. Moon, cloud, _____

7. Tractor, combine, _____

8. Monopoly, Scrabble, _____

9. Shirt, dress, _____

10. Lamb, pony, _____

11. Table, desk, _____

12. Skyscraper, fence post, _____*

*for those brave enough to try

Comment:

The answer to the challenger question must be an object which is vertical, such as a telephone pole, church spire, etc.

A STORY

Materials: Story tape.

Materials: Instruction card.

WHAT WOULD YOU DO?

You have been playing near a creek. Your mother has told you not to play there. But you did anyway, and you have found some crayfish you would like to keep.

In the process of finding them, you slipped just a little bit and got wet. And you were wearing your new shoes. Your mother is going to be furious!

All the other kids get to play by the creek and you think your mother is being too strict. That's why you went to the creek today—all the other kids went. If you had not gone there, the other kids wouldn't like you.

1. What is your *main* problem?

2. What are some of the other problems?

3. Is your mother being fair? Why or why not?

4. What should you do?

Comment:

Again, children are being asked to think logically, sort out the issues, and find solutions.

WEEK 26 ART

Materials: Aluminum foil, tagboard, paper-hole reinforcers, markers, gummed stars and dots, etc., etc.

THIS IS YOUR ROBOT SPEAKING

#$*&!¶ This is robot-talk, and it means: Make a new robot! Your job today is to make any kind of robot you like. Use any materials you think you need to make an interesting automaton (that's another word for robot).

THIS IS YOUR ROBOT SPEAKING

INSTRUCTIONS

Comment:

These instructions are intentionally vague.
Let children go with this one.

Materials: Use Week 3 presentation.

WHAT ABOUT. . . CHALK?

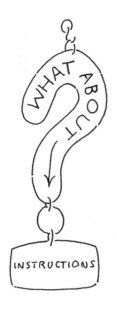

1. Locate the new Childcraft Book 8 called How We Get Things.

2. Read the story on page 231.

3. On your own paper, answer these questions:

   A. What is chalk, really?

   B. In your own words, describe how chalk is made.

   C. Make a list of other materials used for writing.

Comment:

   Keep the subject interesting. Personalize the questions when you can.

Materials: Tagboard.

FIND THE "STREET BEAT"

You are searching for some special words today. Read the story, find all words which rhyme with *street*, and write them in cursive on your own paper. If you finish early, think of other words which rhyme with street.

Our house was neat. But I didn't like the location. It was near a busy street. Believe me, it wasn't a treat to hear those big semi-trailer trucks whizzing by late at night. I often would lie in bed and tap out the number of trucks with my feet.

One summer evening when the heat was especially bad, a water line broke and they blocked off my street. I never had sleep so sweet!

The next morning, I had to eat my words because the water line still wasn't fixed. To be without water is unhandy. You can't get a drink of water, and when you're thirsty, water is hard to beat!

Comment:

Handwriting assignments this late in the year might as well *do* something. This one does.

199

Materials: 3 pencils, shoe box, books, spring scale, 2 long rubber bands, roller skate, string, small sandpaper squares, salad oil in dish, brush, lab sheet and board.

FRICTION

Experiment No. 22—Friction   Name _____

When one thing moves against another thing, there is a force called *friction*. Friction tries to *slow down* things which are moving. If you slide your feet across a carpet, friction is occurring. The roughness of the carpet keeps your feet from moving too fast.

PART 1

1. Working with the box with the books on top, try pulling the box across the table. Read the spring balance as you pull. How many pounds of force were needed to move the box? _____

2. Try putting pencils under the box. Pull the box across the table. How many pounds of force were needed to move the box? _____

3. Try putting the roller skate under the box. (Tie the skate to the box with the string.) How does the box move now? _____

4. Friction was working all three times, but friction was almost "beaten" when:

   _____ I pulled the box myself.

   _____ I put pencils under the box.

   _____ I put a roller skate under the box.

5. Think of how hard it would be to make a car move if it didn't have wheels!

PART 2

6. Now, take the roller skate and two rubber bands and lock the wheels of the skate by crisscrossing the rubber bands on both sides like this: ⟨o⟩⋈⟨o⟩

7. Put the roller skate on the sloping board and notice how hard it is for the roller skate to go down the board. Why? _____

PART 3

8. Take two of the small pieces of sandpaper. Rub the sandy sides together. Does the paper move easily? _____

9. Using the brush, put a coat of oil on the sandy side of both pieces of sandpaper. Now, try rubbing them together. Is the rubbing easier? _____

10. What took the friction away? _____

SPRING BALANCE

Comment: Spring scales (or balances) are easy to get. Try a hardware store. If there is a fisherman in the family, you might be able to borrow his fisherman's scale.

Materials: Catalog, tagboard.

GO TO A SALE!

The sale catalog will be used for this assignment. Answer the questions on your own paper.

1. Find five different kinds of materials used in clothing. (Such as cotton.)

2. Why do many of the items listed say "Limit 1," or "Limit 2"?

3. Find six adjectives and write them along with the nouns they describe.

4. Find synonyms for these words:

   a. variety

   b. large

   c. soft.

5. Find the sentence or phrase which tells how long the sale will last.

6. Where is the store located?

Comment:

   Sale catalogs are no chore to locate these days. Use a "fat" one at this center.

Materials: Tagboard.

PARTS OF SPEECH

Read the clues, then try to think of answers which would fit the number of blanks. All answers deal with parts of speech and other things we have discussed in English. This is hard, but you can do it!

P _ _ _ _ _   More than one.

A _ _ _ _ _ _   Word for opposites.

_ R _ _ _ _ _   Name for words like he, she, you, I.

_ _ _ _ T _ _   A kind of letter you use at the beginning of every sentence.

S _ _ _ _ _ _   Name for a word which means the same as another word.

_ O _ _   Name for person, place, or thing.

F   Freebie!

S _ _ _ _ _ _   Name for the who or what of a sentence.

_ _ _ P _ _ _ _   Two words put together to make one word.

_ E _ _   Name for action or "doing" word.

_ _ _ _ _ _ _ _ E   Name for describing word.

C _ _ _ _   Punctuation mark for pause.

H _ _ _ _ _   Name for words that sound alike but are spelled differently.

Comment:

The answers are: plural, antonym, pronoun, capital, synonym, noun, subject, compound, verb, adjective, comma, and homonym.

Many children will not be able to provide all the answers.

Materials: Tagboard.

PATTERNS

Keep the pattern going. Figure out what is happening, then continue the pattern by making as many figures as you see blanks. Problem one, for instance, should have two answers.

1. △□△□△□ _ _

2. 1 5 9 13 _

3. △□○○△□○○△□○ _ _ _ _ _ _

4. _ \ ⟨ ⟨ ⌒ ⌐ _

5. 1 2 3 5 6 7 9 _ _ _

6. ∪ ∩ ⊔ _

7. ▱ ▱ ▱ ⊠ ⊠ ⊠ ▱ _ _ _ _

8. ◯ ◯ ◯ ◯ ◯ ◯ _ _

9. + + ⊓ + + ⊓ + + _ _

10. 11 22 _ _

11. ⌒∧⌒ ⌒⊓⌒ ⌒∧⌒ _____

12. Goodbye Goodbye _____

Comment:

The patterns are more sophisticated this time, except for number one and number twelve.

Materials: Teacher-made tape.

LISTENING MIX-UP

SCRIPT FOR WEEK 27

(One-minute music fade-in) Hello, boys and girls. For once, I'm going to tell you *not* to do something. Today, *do not* number your paper in advance. Next, I'm going to tell you *not* to do something else. I do not want you to stop the tape to do your writing today, or to rerun the tape. Because, this listening assignment requires you to do your fastest thinking. As usual, you must listen carefully. Are you ready? Here we go. Write number one on your paper. (Pause) Now, I am going to say two words. When I say them, you are to write and keep writing anything and everything you can possibly think of about these two words. Keep writing and writing and, if you run out of ideas, just write your own name over and over until you can think of more ideas. For instance, if I say firecracker, I might write the words hot, used on the Fourth of July, my sister got one once, they are very stinky, cylinders, red, fuse, I hate them, loud noise and on and on. Do you understand? Are you ready for number one? Here it is. Keep writing until I say stop. *Fire hydrant*. Begin writing. (Pause for one minute) Stop. Number two. Again, keep writing until I say stop. The subject is. . . *handles*. Begin writing. (Pause for one minute) Stop. The next few problems will be questions. Will you please just answer the question? Number three. Name one animal which lives in Australia. (Pause) Number four. Name the vice-president of the United States. (Pause) Number five. What is a feline? (Pause)

Number six. What is a canine? (Pause) Number seven. Give me an antonym, which is an opposite, for the word tall. (Pause) Number eight. An antonym for the word dark. (Pause) Number nine. An antonym for the word everything. (Pause) Number ten. An antonym for the word smart. (Pause) Number eleven. A synonym for the word fat. (Pause) The next three sentences I will say to you are unfinished. They need to be completed in a way that is as colorful and interesting as you can make them. Number twelve. The sentence is: The wind was as cold as. . . (Pause) Number thirteen. The baby's skin was softer than. . . (Pause) Number fourteen. The old pig looked fatter than. . . (Pause) Now, answer the rest of the questions as fast as you can. Number fifteen. What is two times two times two take away three? (Pause) I'll repeat. What is two times two times two take away three? (Pause) Number sixteen. What color are toenails? (Pause) Number seventeen. Who is the President of the United States? (Pause) Number eighteen. Put your name in the lower left-hand corner of your paper. (Pause) Number nineteen is one of those write-as-much-as-you-can-and-keep-writing assignments again, and this is the last thing you do today at this center. The words are. . . *summer evening*. Write everything you can about a summer evening —what it smells like, what you do, where you go and so forth. Do this now. (Two-minute pause) Stop. You've done a good job. Good listening and good day. (One-minute music fade-out)

Comment:

This can be a lively listening project. Do not go too fast with your directions.

The sustained writing task is limited to one minute at first, allowing children to get warmed up, and finishes with a two-minute assignment.

In reality, two minutes of sustained writing is quite a long time.

WRITE A POEM, WRITE A POEM

Materials: Tagboard.

Below is a poem. Notice that every other line is the same.

> It is noisy
> on the bus.
> Bumpy riding
> on the bus.
> Stopping and starting
> on the bus.
> People squeezed together
> on the bus.

Now, your job is to write another poem with every other line the same. The lines in your poem which should be the same are: *in my hair* or *in the morning*. Make your poem as long as you wish. If you have time, try some other poems, making up your own repeated lines.

Comment:

Again, children are playing with rhythms and cadences— and, it's easy. These poems should be read aloud and savored.

DO YOUR OWN THING

Materials: White paper, black marker.

Today, you can draw *anything* you like—as long as you keep the picture black and white. Use the black marker. Have fun, and do what you want to do!

Comment:

When you introduce centers on Monday, pick up one of the large white sheets of paper and, with marker in hand, make a bold, irreverent mark on the page. Let children know they can draw anything. And talk about filling up the whole paper.

If a child wants to use crayons for this assignment, tell him no.

Materials: 21 note cards.

THE TRUE AND NOT-SO-TRUE

On your own paper, number from 1 to 20 and write true or false.

1. A small boy can run as fast as a horse.

2. (Your principal) has grey hair.

3. The sun looks brighter in the sky than the moon.

4. Tulips grow higher than sunflowers.

5. A group of birds is called a flock.

6. A group of cows is called a pack.

7. You usually grow more on your birthday than any other day.

8. Paper comes from trees.

9. Elephants are larger than lions.

10. There are sixty seconds in one hour.

11. There are seven openings in your head.

12. (Your school) is in the northwest part of the city.

13. Gravy is made with vinegar and honey.

14. Corn grows naturally in rows.

15. Fossils are inside all rocks.

16. The opposite of south is north.

17. Eighteen months is the same as two years.

18. 380 comes before 479.

19. Robbers always wear eye masks.

20. Gold is a precious metal.

Comment:

Put your directions and the individual sentences on note cards.

Materials: Tagboard.

OLD-FASHIONED CURES

In pioneer days, people had to figure out ways to help themselves when they were sick or had problems. Read the three cures. Then write in cursive the one which you find most interesting.

1. *The Nose-Bleed Cure.* A simple cure for nose-bleed is to crowd the fingers tight into the ears and chew, pressing the teeth well together, as if chewing food.

2. *The Ear-Ache Cure.* Take a large onion and cut it into slices. Put a slice of onion, then a slice of strong tobacco, then a slice of onion again, then tobacco. Cook over fire until onion is tender, press out the juice and drop into the ear. Gives instant relief.

3. *Hiccups.* Make white sugar wet by adding cider vinegar. Give an infant a few grains of the vinegar sugar. The effect will be noticed immediately.

Comment:

Emphasize that children should not try these cures since they were home remedies and may not have worked at all.

This assignment gives youngsters a certain perspective on how their ancestors faced several problems. This may lead to a discussion on modern-day home remedies, such as methods to cure hiccups.

Materials: Petroleum jelly, newspapers, carbon paper, spoon,
leaves, lab sheet, paper plate.

LOOK AT A LEAF

Experiment No. 23—Looking at a Leaf   Name _____

From the box, choose one leaf which interests you. Study it carefully. Then do the following:

1. What colors do you see in your leaf? _____

2. Notice that one side is rougher than the other. Why is this? _____

_____

3. You are going to make a print which will show the vein pattern of your leaf, so cover the vein side with the petroleum jelly. (Remember, the vein side is the bumpy side.) Be sure to cover every bit of that side with the jelly. Use your finger.

4. On the padding of newspapers, place your leaf so that the *greasy side is up*. This means you will be looking at the vein side.

5. Lay the carbon paper on top of your leaf so that the dark side of the carbon paper is down. This means that the dark side is touching your leaf, and the light side of the carbon paper is up.

6. Using the back of the spoon, rub across the carbon paper several times. You are inking your leaf.

7. Remove the carbon paper and throw it away. Throw away any greasy newspaper, also.

8. Place your "inked" leaf (greasy side down) on a piece of white paper which has been put on top of the newspaper pad.

9. Cover with another piece of paper.

10. Rub the top paper with the spoon.

11. Carefully remove the top paper and the leaf and you'll find a print of your leaf!

12. Put it on the windowsill to dry.

Comment: Cut a number of small carbon-paper squares. Provide plenty of newspapers so that children will have a "printing pad." Use porous paper for the actual print (newsprint or construction paper). Have a wastebasket at the center. Some paper towels are needed, also.

You may want to run through the leaf-printing process on Monday, although most children can follow these directions on their own.

Materials: Book. Use Week 17
presentation from Language Arts.

A BOOKLOOK

Use the book and follow directions carefully.

1. Turn to page 168. Write the first three words in the second paragraph.

2. On page 59, the first complete paragraph begins with the word *young*. With what word does the fifth paragraph end?

3. How many chapters are in this book?

4. Write the title of the eighth chapter.

5. On page 103, you'll find the word *capacity* in the third paragraph. Can you guess its meaning, letting the words around it help you?

6. Who is the author of this book?

7. How many pages are in the first chapter?

8. How many pages are in the whole book?

Comment:

Tasks may seem inconsequential, but the objectives are important: to give practice in following directions and to gain general information about how to use books.

An adult book works best for this project. Your questions, of course, will be different.

Materials: Use Week 4 presentation.

WHAT AM I?

INSTRUCTIONS

Figure out the word letter by letter first, then number 1 to 3 on your own paper.

I'm in stamp but not mats.

I'm in bread but not bead.

I'm in leaf but not loaf.

I'm in jam but not ham.

I'm in pull but not pill.

I'm in drink but not brink.

I'm in wide but not wade.

I'm in cash but not shag.

I'm in sent but not tons.

1. What am I?

2. If I would say that I'm prejudiced against dogs with long ears, would you know what prejudice means? Write what you think it means.

3. Now, look up the word in the dictionary. Then answer this question: Is prejudice good or bad? Why? (Two parts to this question).

Comment:

The answer is prejudice. Even though the answer is tipped off in the second question, children usually don't read ahead.

Materials: 12 word cards, instruction card.

NONSENSE WORDS

Some nonsense words are on the cards. You are to group them in different ways. When you have arranged them according to one idea, write down the way you grouped them and the words that you used. Then, think of another way to group them. Write that idea, too. The example should help you understand.

Example: All four-letter words

1. grun

2. dlur

3. glib

4. bznn

5. lwpp

glib	grun	bznn	bot
mux	dlur	lwpp	fon
klib	hib	frx	yok

Comment:

Put the nonsense words and the directions on separate 3 x 5-inch note cards. Children will then be able to move the cards into various groupings.

A STORY

Materials: Story tape.

WEEK 28 CREATIVE WRITING

Materials: String hook-up, old clock with instructions taped on it, adding machine tape.

CREATIVE LISTENING

On the adding machine paper, list every sound you hear in a ten-minute period. After the ten minutes are over, go back and underline all words with two syllables.

Comment:

There is time to include the syllabication work. In this case, the added complexity doesn't hurt the first part of the activity. Tape your directions to an old clock.

WEEK 28   ART

Materials: White paper plates, yarn, crayons, assorted materials.

LET'S FACE IT!

Have you ever seen someone with a face as round as a paper plate? Probably not. Faces come in all shapes, don't they?

Well, since there aren't any real people who have circles for faces, let's make a make-believe one. Start with a paper plate. Then use construction paper, markers, crayons, or any other materials. Make the face happy, mad, dumb, sad. . . you decide what your person will look like.

Comment:

If you are predisposed to dislike smiley faces, mention to the children that they ought to stay away from such gimmicks.

The faces needn't be flat. Paper can be folded to make noses and eyelids. Yarn or curled construction paper makes good hair.

212

BY CHILDREN FOR CHILDREN

Materials: Contributor's page from children's magazine, tagboard.

1. Who drew the dinosaur?

2. What do you think the three objects are that Nathan drew?

3. What do you think Mona Morris drew?

4. Where does it say to send pictures which you have made?

5. What is your favorite picture and why?

6. How old is Michele?

7. Write a sentence describing John's picture.

Comment: Use a contributor's page from a children's magazine again this week.

I DON'T LIKE. . .

Materials: Tagboard.

Copy the sentences in cursive, filling in the blanks with words which would fit. Sentences can be serious or silly. No proper names, please.

1. I don't like _____ in my _____.

2. I don't like _____ on my _____.

3. I don't like _____ with lots of _____.

4. I don't like _____ and _____.

5. I don't like _____ on top of my _____.

6. I don't like _____ under my _____.

Comment:

The admonition about proper nouns comes from experience. Children will use other children's names in some of the blanks if not deterred.

213

Materials: Flowers, black paper, picture card, cellophane tape, lab sheet, paper plate.

PARTS OF A FLOWER

Experiment No. 24 — Parts of a Flower   Name_____

Choose one flower. You will be working with it for this experiment. Next, get ready to be a surgeon. But you will not be using a scalpel, you will be using your fingers. You are going to take apart the flower and find all the important parts.

The picture on the card will help you to identify the parts.

1. Pull out the stamens and count them. How many does your flower have? _____

2. Take one of the stamens and rub it across the piece of black paper. What happens? _____

3. Tape your other stamens right here.

4. Find the pistil. Tape it here.

5. Take off the sepals. How many do you find? _____

6. Are the sepals above or below the petals? _____

7. Tape the sepals here.

8. Now, take off the petals. How many petals are on your flower? _____ What color are they? _____

9. Tape your petals here (or at the bottom of the page).

10. Find the receptacle. What color is it? _____ Tape your receptacle here.

STAMENS

PETALS

PISTIL

SEPALS

RECEPTACLE

Comment:

Probably the easiest and best flower to use for this activity is the tulip. The parts are relatively large and simple.
Be sure to provide a card showing the flower parts.
You may wish to have a magnifying glass at this center this week, also.

WHITE!

Materials: White tagboard, dictionary.

There are many expressions which begin with the word white. First, look up the word white in the dictionary and answer these questions. All underlined words are in the dictionary.

1. If I bought a white elephant, what would that mean? (meaning 2)

2. What kind of creature might appear in white-face in a circus? (meaning 2)

3. If my husband were invited to a white-tie dinner, what kind of dinner would it be?

4. Think of one or two objects which might be in a white sale.

5. If a recipe calls for white sauce, what kind of ingredients do I need?

6. Who lives in the White House?

7. If some soldiers showed a white flag, what would that mean? (meaning 1)

8. What part of a car is called a white-wall?

9. Would white water be choppy or calm?

10. What is a white throat?

Comment:

Not every child will come up with all the right answers. Some will. Every student, however, will be looking in the dictionary, not only for entries but also for various meanings—and this is the objective. The second objective is no less important—to get children hooked on the colorful expressions in the English language.

Your questions may be slightly different, depending on the dictionary you use.

Materials: Tagboard.

WHO GOOFED?

Read the four sentences. Then change the homonyms to make the sentences *write*! *Right* on your own paper.

1. Eye read in the paper wear he went two the sail.

2. Eye tot my dog two fetch.

3. The soar will heel in a weak oar to.

4. Wood you sea if my glasses are their?

If time remains, think of other homonyms and make other sentences.

Comment:

Homonyms are only fun if they're used incorrectly in sentences. Children respond to mistakes.

Materials: Colored worksheet.

CATEGORIES

Directions: Fill in as many of the boxes as you can by looking at the top of the column for the topic and to the left of each row for the beginning letter of the word you will be making. The example will help you.

	TV character	Fruit or vegetable	Flower	Type of drink
G	*Gomer*	*grape*		
R				
O				
W				
S				

Comment:

The children shouldn't have problems coming up with ideas in these four subject areas. The beginning letter restriction *does* make the assignment more complicated, however. The majority of youngsters will do very well.

Materials: Teacher-made tape.

GETTING PLACES

SCRIPT FOR WEEK 29

(One-minute music fade-in) Hello. Today, we're going to get to the very bottom of things. . . really, the bottom. Because we are going to be thinking about the very tips of our bodies. More specifically, we're going to be thinking about those things we stand on. . . our feet. Granted, we were born barefooted, but before too long, our mothers covered us with that first foot dressing called the bootie. When you think of it, we wore a variety of things on our feet as we grew older, didn't we? Beside number one on your paper, try to make a long list of everything people can put on their feet. It helps if you think of different kinds of jobs and activities in order to come up with something other than just shoes. Think, too, of foreign countries. What do people wear in Holland, for instance? Do your writing now. (Pause) Next, I have a very special request. I want you to stop the tape and walk all the way around the room, taking *regular* steps. Count how many steps it takes you as you circle the room. Write the number beside number two on your paper. (Pause) Probably, some of you tried to make long steps just now, even though I asked you to take regular steps. I can understand that it would be tempting to try to circle the room in as few steps as possible. Which brings me to another idea. How many ways are there to move around on our feet? List the different ways you can move your feet—without the help of roller skates or any other device. Skipping would be one way. What are other ways? Do this work for number three now. (Pause) Speaking of moving, I now want you to count the number of giant steps it takes you to get down to the office door and back. Do not run. Do not make any noise. Put the number of steps beside number four when you get back. Do rewind the tape before you go. Thank you, happy listening, good day.

Comment:

This activity meanders pleasantly.

Materials: Tagboard.

TALL TALES

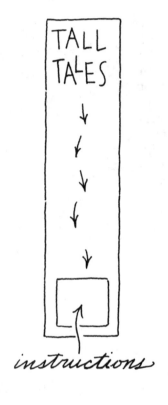

All the boys in third grade in (your school) have to get their heads shaved when they reach nine years of age. After that, they wear wigs made out of dogs' tails. One boy took a trip to Florida to see his grandmother and wagged his head so hard, his wig fell off!

All the girls in third grade in (your school) have to wear tomato sauce smeared on their elbows so that the sunlight won't ever get on them. One girl decided to wash her right elbow and see what was underneath, and when she saw, she fainted!

Read the two tall tales. Now it's your turn to write a tall tale about:

1. A bat, bubble bath and hair.

2. A strong man, the world and a tree.

3. Or, make up your own.

Comment:

When you have a tall tale to tell, make it taller! The two examples provide quite ample stimulation. The suggested components are put in for the benefit of slow starters. Many other children will use their own ideas and be off at a gallop.

Materials: Pencil, paper.

ART LINES

When most of us think about making a drawing, we think about drawing *things*—a dog, a cat, a person. Did you ever stop to think it might be possible to express an idea with *just a line*? Look at this line, and then decide which of the three words fits it best.

bouncy
sad
calm

The best answer probably would be *bouncy*, wouldn't it?

Now, number your paper from 1 to 15. Leave plenty of space between the numbers. Next to each number, make a line that describes the word.

1. fast

2. slow

3. smooth

4. rough

5. happy

6. funny

7. light

8. heavy

9. nervous

10. hop

11. loop

12. stormy

13. mad

14. cute

15. sick

Comment:

Probably you should do a little coaching when you introduce the centers on Monday. A couple of lines drawn on the blackboard will help reinforce the written instructions.

You might mention the fact that music is another way of expressing ideas, moods, and emotions without actually describing them in words or pictures.

Materials: Travel brochure, tag-board.

BELIEVE IT OR NOT

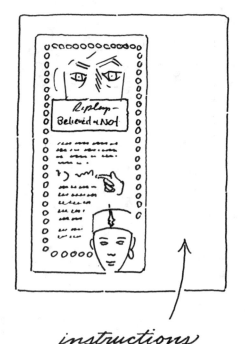

instructions

1. How many exhibits at Ripley's Museum?

2. Ripley's full name was _____.

3. He traveled in how many countries?

4. What is strange about the man who is pictured?

5. Name two exhibits and tell about them.

6. Where is the museum located?

Comment:

This is merely a model for what you will be doing. First, go to a travel bureau and pick up several free travel brochures. Then, take the most interesting brochure apart and paste it to tagboard.

Frame your questions from the information given and you'll have a lively center.

I chose a Ripley's Believe It or Not brochure because I knew I couldn't miss with that kind of subject matter.

Materials: Tagboard.

TEN FACTS ABOUT A LITTLE BIT OF EVERYTHING

1. Hummingbirds have a poor sense of smell and don't care about sweet-smelling flowers. Instead, they are attracted by color.

2. You can tell the sex of an Eastern box turtle by the color of its eyes. A male has red eyes, a female has brown eyes.

3. The female bullfrog is larger than the male bullfrog.

4. A honeybee which has found food puts on a dance when it returns to the hive to tell other bees about it.

5. When deer shed their antlers in the winter, it doesn't cause them any pain.

6. Owls sleep by closing their eyes from the bottom up.

7. Elephants often die from a narrowing of the blood vessels—which can cause death in man, too.

8. Before we learned how to get sugar from the sugar beet and sugar cane, things were sweetened with honey.

9. Dolphins sometimes will go to the aid of wounded dolphins, holding the wounded dolphin's head above water so it can breathe.

10. If a snake accidentally swallows its own poison, it won't get sick.

In cursive, follow these directions.

1. Write the fact you found most interesting. Copy it just as it is written, in your best cursive.

2. Now, in your own words, tell why that fact was the most interesting to you.

3. Are there any facts you knew before you read them today? List by number the facts you already knew.

4. What is the smallest animal discussed in the ten facts today?

5. What is the largest animal which is mentioned?

Comment:

This "shotgun" approach always works.

221

Materials: Lightweight paper, paper clips, tape, two paper plates.

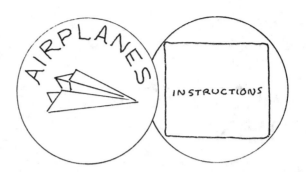

BE AN AERONAUTICAL ENGINEER!

Your project today in science is to be an engineer. No, you're not going to be a train engineer. You are going to be an *aeronautical engineer,* which means, simply—an airplane designer!

You are going to make two paper airplanes. One should be designed so that it flies as far as possible. The other should be designed to fly as gracefully as possible and do dives and loops.

You may use four sheets of paper. This gives you a practice piece for each airplane. You may use paper clips or whatever kind of weight you wish. Use tape if you need it.

You may decorate your plane, also.

You can test-fly your airplanes in the back of the room by the closet *if* you can do so gently and quietly.

Next week, we will have an airplane-flying contest. Work hard, and the best of luck!

Comment:

Since this is the final week in the learning center program, the airplane-designing contest, though marginally scientific in nature, will be the culminating activity.

Few children, if any, will be helpless when it comes to making the airplanes. Most children will relish the chance.

The majority of youngsters will not have time to decorate their airplanes in twenty minutes. Permit them to do this in their spare time.

On the day of the big contest, your judges will come from students who were absent or did not make an airplane.

Conduct the contest in the school gym.

Materials: Tagboard, atlas.

USING THE ATLAS

Find the map of the world in the atlas. Then, follow these directions.

1. Write three of the biggest cities you can find.

2. Name three countries in Europe.

3. Write the names of three rivers in the United States.

4. List as many mountain chains as you can find.

5. If you could go anywhere in the world, where would you go? Why?

Comment:

   This project has been included because children have not yet worked with an atlas at this center. They should get familiar with this book.

Materials: Book, tagboard.

ON PAGE 44. . .

ON PAGE 44

INSTRUCTIONS

Using the book provided for you at this center, follow these instructions:

1. On page 44, list three pronouns.

2. On page 79, list three proper nouns.

3. Find a question on page 111 and write it.

4. In the second paragraph on page 39, there is a sentence which uses an exclamation point. Find it and write it!

5. Choose two nouns on page 71.

6. Find three adverbs (words which describe the verb and usually end in ly) on page 52.

7. Close the book.

8. Quit.

Comment:

Well, do they know it by now or don't they? From this exercise, you will get a good idea about whether they can identify nouns, pronouns, etc.

PRIBBLES AND ZASTERS

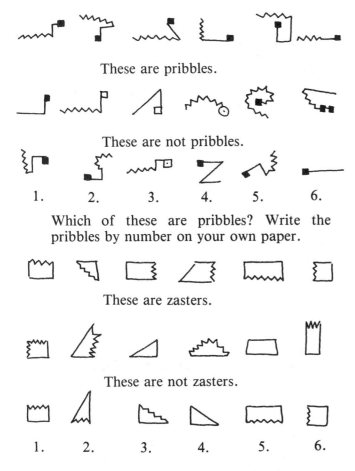

These are pribbles.

These are not pribbles.

1.   2.   3.   4.   5.   6.

Which of these are pribbles? Write the pribbles by number on your own paper.

These are zasters.

These are not zasters.

1.   2.   3.   4.   5.   6.

Which of these are zasters? Write the zasters by number on your own paper.

If there is time, make other zasters and pribbles—using the same ideas which have been given.

Comment:

Pribbles and zasters present the most difficult classification challenges in this series.

Pribbles have wavy-straight lines and dark square heads.

Zasters have one wavy side and are all the same height. The latter will be hard for many children to recognize, since this is a "new" property.

The answers are: Pribbles are 1, 2, 5. Zasters are 1, 3, 5, 6.

A STORY

Materials: Tagboard.

THE DRAGON'S ELBOWS

Write a story using these words: dragon, girl, elbows, burped, cookies, polka-dotted, mouth, fat, mouse.

All words can be used more than once and the endings may change. This means you could write *burping* as well as *burped*!

Comment:

You will be surprised at the results of this seemingly simple assignment. No two stories will be the same, and some will be quite ingenious.

HOW DOES YOUR GARDEN GROW?

WEEK 30   ART

Materials: Colored paper, scissors, paste, markers.

It's spring and school is about over. Hooray! Let's get into the spring spirit by making a class flower garden. Use the construction paper to cut out parts of a flower. (Remember our science center about flowers?) When your flower parts are cut out, paste them together and add your flower (or flowers) to our garden. (You can make an imaginary flower if you like.)

Comment:

This could be a good bulletin board project. If your board is occupied, provide another display area for your young gardeners.

Materials: Book on reptiles. Use Week 3 presentation.

WHAT ABOUT. . . THE COBRA?

1. Pick up the book on snakes at this center and take it to your desk.

2. Turn to page 28 and read about the cobra.

3. Then, answer these questions.
   A. Where is the snake found?
   B. What does it do when it is excited?
   C. What does *venomous* mean?

4. Next, read page 37. Write two differences between snakes and lizards.

   D. One difference is. . .
   E. Another difference is. . .

Comment:

   Never underestimate the power of snakes, lizards and other creepy things. Children like reading about them.

Index